GROWING YOUR OWN FOOD IN HONG KONG

BY THE SAME AUTHOR

Urban Gardening for Hong Kong (1983)

Urban Gardening: A Hong Kong Gardener's Journal (2006)

Growing Your Own Food in Hong Kong

(Expanded Edition)

By Arthur van Langenberg

Photographs by the author

The Chinese University Press

Growing Your Own Food in Hong Kong *(Expanded Edition)*
By Arthur van Langenberg

ISBN: 978-962-996-647-8

First Edition 2013
Expanded Edition 2015

Published by The Chinese University Press
The Chinese University of Hong Kong
Sha Tin, N.T., Hong Kong
Fax: +852 2603 7355
E-mail: cup@cuhk.edu.hk
Website: www.chineseupress.com

Printed in Hong Kong

"It is good that my heart can feel the simple and innocent pleasures a man knows when the cabbage he eats at the table is the one that he grew himself, the pleasure he takes not only in eating the cabbage but in remembering all those good days, the fine morning he planted it, the mellow evenings he watered it and the delight he felt in its daily growth."

Johann Wolfgang von Goethe
The Sorrows of Young Werther (1774)

CONTENTS

Preface to the Expanded Edition

Some years ago I was foolhardy enough to contemplate a book about growing one's own food in Hong Kong, a city renowned for its surfeit of concrete and its plethora of eating venues to suit every taste and pocket. Surely I would be sowing seed on stony ground. After plunging headlong nonetheless, I had no choice but to sit back to await results. Well, I was amazed by the number of people who admitted stirrings of their latent gardening juices, responding to my message that growing your own food, even in the smallest way, is more than just planting a few seeds—it is a way of life. The greatest surprise was the number of start-ups among people who had no previous experience of growing anything: most have expressed delight in their new venture. Another unexpected turn of events was the interest generated among gardeners outside of Hong Kong. It seems the book has proved useful to gardeners in those areas around the world with subtropical climates similar to ours. This was indeed an interesting development.

I have also been pleasantly surprised when approached by total strangers, from the humblest to the grandest, who want to talk about growing food. The exchange is often two-way: many passers-by, gardeners themselves or those who had been farmers in days past, have added to my knowledge of growing vegetables, which often involves the swapping of seeds, plants and opinions. While growing flowers and ornamental shrubs has always been a genteel pastime, the growing of food was thoughtlessly left to the faceless, seldom-regarded, lowly-paid grunts known as farmers. All that mattered was for food to appear in the markets or on shop shelves, neatly packaged but from where we know not. It may not be generally known that fully one-third of all food produced ends up as garbage. We are sorely in need of a change of mindset.

Despite some alterations and additions, this 2015 revision does not alter the structure or the tone of the book in any way. My message also remains unchanged: to cultivate a garden is to harvest knowledge. Discover the miracle of life.

Arthur van Langenberg (2014)

Preface to the First Edition

One reason for growing your own food is to bring you back to basics. City dwellers have largely suffered a disconnect from Nature, believing, firstly, that there is very little of Nature around them, and, secondly, that they have never had the incentive to grow anything. On the first count they should be reminded that in this very built-up city of ours, the surprising fact is that three quarters of the land area is occupied by countryside. On the second count—well, that is the reason for this book, to provide that incentive by pointing out the possibilities. One of these possibilities is to take active steps to bring Nature back into your living environment, space limitations notwithstanding.

The modern consumer, spoilt for choice, demands instant gratification: winter vegetables in the summer, summer squash in the winter. And he is indulged by globalisation. Food from halfway around the globe arrives by jet aircraft, perhaps over the Arctic Circle, all the while spewing carbon and toxic gases into the earth's atmosphere. Food mileage leaves a massive carbon footprint.

Mass-produced food is dominated by the need to raise flawless merchandise in the least possible time, requirements that can only be met by the heavy use of chemical fertilisers, pesticides and technological manipulation. The run-off into our waterways of nitrogen from fertilisers has already destroyed much of the ecology of our river systems and oceans. Yet only the tiniest minority of shoppers will dwell on the provenance of their purchases, and even less on how that food is produced, packaged and transported. The final choice is dependent solely on the personal and prosaic taste of the purchaser.

Growing your own food deals with some of the above objections. Very few, if any of us, will be able to be self-sufficient in vegetables; but even if you grow a small fraction of what you need, the satisfaction is there, that you are doing the right thing. No pesticides or strong chemical fertilisers means unadulterated, safe food. Tastier for its not having been harvested six months ago, and eaten instead, fresh-picked, before the crunch is gone or the sugars are lost. Just as important is the satisfaction of watching the day-to-day changes in the plants as they grow, always demanding something of you, always reacting to what you do, affecting the very rhythm of your life. Not least, it brings back the wonder and the anticipation of the seasons, each with its own bounty, increasing the value we place on our food.

To cultivate a garden is to harvest knowledge. Growing your own food is a multi-dimensional activity. It connects you to botany, entomology, meteorology, chemistry, medicine, geology, ornithology, philosophy and much else, each one urging you to explore a little further. Mathematics? The arrangement of leaves on a stem or the pattern seen on seed heads has a definite relation to mathematical principles such as Fibonacci numbers. Look at a sunflower head and try to find out more.

It has not escaped me that not all of us can—or should—grow our own food. The exigencies of modern living can prohibit even the most willing, while here in cramped Hong Kong, only a very few have gardens. I regard my tiny garden plot, all 25 square metres of it, as beyond value, my own little piece of the promised land. The rest of my gardening is done entirely in containers.

Let me do my best to show you how a rooftop, a balcony, a windowsill, a wall, a fence, or a few flower pots, is all that you need to send you on your way.

You will make another great discovery: growing your own food is fun!

Arthur van Langenberg (2012)

Foreword to the Expanded Edition

看書，是和作者的心靈交流，是了解和吸收他的學識和經驗。如果作者是你認識和尊敬的，你當然會更享受書中的樂趣。我說的當然是看梁雅達醫生的這本書。此書記載了本地種到的、可吃的植物。由於非常暢銷，現今已經推出這第二版。

我承認自己是非常喜歡胡亂種些東西玩玩的人，不能算是園藝。梁雅達醫生就可當之而無愧。我曾說他是當今的城市園藝大師，他身為資深外科醫生，但對本地各種植物認識之深，已經到了專家的境界，其中包括花草樹木，及可吃的植物，都寫在他的兩本書內。第一本*Urban Gardening* 說本地的植物，包括觀賞和食用的，想許多人都看過。

梁醫生對吃的研究也不簡單。我最享受是和他一起吃，因為會吃到一些新口味，和學到一些以前不知道原來可以吃的東西。一次在他家花園喝下午茶。他隨手在田裏摘了些植物來做沙律吃，很可口。原來野草般的松葉牡丹，及金蓮花的花和葉是可以生吃的。他說很多花都可以吃，包括菊花、秋海棠、玫瑰、萬壽菊，甚至南瓜花及雄性的木瓜花，都是最好的美味。不用擔心怎樣弄來吃，他在書內有詳細的介紹。

梁醫生家的花園，也令人大開眼界。他能巧妙地善用他家旁邊的空地甚至大廈樓底的地基位置，把這些本來沒用的地方都種滿植物。春天到來，到處繁花似錦，非常美觀。他種的除了常見的花草蔬果外，還有很少人在家中花園種的玉米、甘蔗，甚至稻米。他書內描述的植物及相片全都是自己種出而拍攝的，非常珍貴。

全書以優美的英文寫成，看時像一邊聽故事，一邊吸收知識，一點也不沉悶。此次第二版又增加了很多有趣的資料，如介紹種植有檸檬味的天竺葵、佛手瓜、火龍果、新品種的番茄、本地的小白菜、牛油果、蒔蘿、木耳、玉米及向日葵等等。未成熟的番茄原來可省回來，製成調味醬；還有番薯怎樣從原產地巴西經葡萄牙到澳門，再由明代大科學家徐光啟引入中國種植的歷史等，並同樣引人入勝。

現在我們的下一代，人人豐衣足食，食物得來太易，所以很少人會知道蔬菜是怎樣來的。我們應跟從此書的指導，由最易種的白菜及菜心起，教小孩種菜，啟發他們對植物的興趣，認識到由種子到整棵菜的長成，是經過了不少辛勞的成果。由此了解到生命的循環，亦學會了尊重食物，不會隨便浪費。

關寶源醫生 全科醫生 (2014)

Foreword to the Expanded Edition

It is with great pleasure that I write this foreword for the launch of the second edition of a book which encourages people to grow their own food at home and is authored by my most honoured teacher and friend, Dr Arthur van Langenberg. I have known Arthur for forty-five years, ever since I was a student in medical school. At that time he was my teacher in surgery and now he is my teacher in gardening. He has a great depth of gardening knowledge and specialises in nurturing plants suitable for urban Hong Kong's environment, for the dual purposes of enjoyment and growing food.

When I first visited Arthur's garden I was amazed to find how he had transformed the concrete surroundings of his home into a garden and a "microfarm" for growing various types of plants, even plants rarely grown in home gardens such as sugar cane, maize and rice. The images found in this book feature all of the plants grown and photographed by Arthur himself.

In this new edition, he has included new plants: chayote, dill, wood ear fungus, dragon fruit, cabbage and local pak choi, as well as an interesting history of how the sweet potato was introduced into China from Brazil via Macao. Arthur also provides suggestions of the various ways of using self-grown products as cooking ingredients to create delicious meals because he believes that eating these plants is an effective way of ensuring a healthy life. More important, the book also emphasises that getting children interested in growing their own food is an integral part of a good education, which makes them realise that food on one's table is the result of hard work and must not be wasted.

Dr Kwan Po Yuen (2014)
General medical practitioner and avid gardener

Foreword to the First Edition

Living off the land ... What an appealing idea! Recent years have seen a widespread boom in raising one's own vegetables on a small or large scale. Increasing concern about the quality of commercial crops, economic necessity and the need to fill spare time have spurred people in Europe and North America into trying to produce at least some of the food that they eat. In the heart of Tokyo, rooftops have been sprouting rice; Parisians are raising fruit trees on their balconies; and even in densely crowded Hong Kong, every year sees more people discovering the pleasure of tending a pot of herbs or a trough of their very own lettuce. Some have taken advantage of opportunities to cultivate a small plot of land in one of the community farms in the New Territories. Even in the heart of Sheung Wan and Kwun Tong you can have your own micro-garden.

Few Hong Kong gardeners will be aiming at self-sufficiency, but everyone needs some guidance on how and where to start. Whether you are fortunate enough to have your own patch of soil or are using containers, this book leads you through the entire process. From the basic growing medium to different types of pots and containers, fertilisers, water and compost, it is all here. Everything is geared to Hong Kong conditions as Arthur suggests the right seed for the right season, how to get it off to a good start and ensure that it reaches maturity. There are even recipes to help you enjoy your harvest to the full. The helpful photographs are all taken by Arthur in his own garden.

Looking at our green hillsides, colourful parks and luxuriant roadside plantings, it might seem that Hong Kong is a gardener's paradise. The answer, as so often, must be both yes and no. And, as in most other things, the Hong Kong way in gardening is a little different. This is why you need some expert guidance. Arthur's third book, *Growing Your Own Food in Hong Kong*, is most timely. True to his training as a surgeon, he has kept meticulous notes on everything that he has ever grown and this is why his text is so authoritative. He makes no assumptions, he is never patronising, but he is there to help you get it right first time. Even if you are not planning your own microfarm, this book just might inspire you to start thinking about it. He enjoys writing almost as much as he enjoys gardening: armchair gardeners will certainly appreciate his enthusiasm and knowledge and his occasional flashes of gentle humour. Suffice it to say that I laughed out loud at one point as I read the text.

Arthur broke new ground with his first book, *Urban Gardening for Hong Kong*, published in 1983. His second book, *Urban Gardening: A Hong Kong Gardener's Journal*, published by The Chinese University Press in 2006, was a much expanded version of the original book. Both books filled a vacuum for Hong Kong gardeners as virtually nothing had been published on this topic in English since Tutcher's slim volume over a century ago. Gardening is the new cooking in Britain these days where a new book (or TV programme) on the topic is launched almost weekly if not daily. In Hong Kong, however, we face a dearth of English-language books geared specifically to local conditions. And I understand the situation is not much better for those who read Chinese.

When I started trying to get things to grow in Hong Kong I was only interested in flowering plants. I was fortunate in having a knowledgeable friend to whom I could turn when I needed advice on where and how to try raising my latest enthusiasm. She has long since gone to the great garden in the sky, but her advice stays with me and my garden still benefits from the fruits of her knowledge.

Arthur's first book was published around the time that I graduated to a real garden and I found it invaluable. When his second book was published, it felt as though we were long-time friends already although at the time we had still never met face to face. We soon remedied that omission and our earlier "literary" friendship was transformed into the special blend of camaraderie that unites everyone who spends time enjoying and working with plants and soil. I have been fortunate enough to visit Arthur's garden and to sample the fruits of his labours on a number of occasions. I am always filled with admiration at what he achieves in the face of seemingly impossible odds. A car park? A concrete bed? A narrow wrap-around terrace? How does he grow so much, so successfully in conditions that most people would dismiss as the city equivalent of an inhospitable desert? This book tells you how, and much more besides. Arthur is the most generous of men and in this volume, as in all his books, he enjoys sharing his acquired knowledge as happily as he shares his seeds, seedlings, cuttings and delicious fresh produce. This is truly a hands-on book as Arthur bases his writing on what he has actually grown.

When Arthur rather hesitantly passed me a draft of the current book, I read it with great excitement. Through our website, the Hong Kong Gardening Society (HKGS) receives a steady flow of enquiries about gardening basics. Those seeking guidance are mostly novices. Others are experienced gardeners accustomed to different climates and they find it hard to source supplies or to get used to the idea that seeds for a European spring sowing should be sown in Hong Kong's autumn. These days the emphasis of our enquiries is shifting from ornamental to edible plants. HKGS does occasionally organise classes and demonstrations for our members, but it is hard to find someone willing to leave their own plants for long enough to conduct a session (which can only cater to a small number of people). It has always been my pleasure to advise people to buy *Urban Gardening* where they will find everything they need. This new book takes us all many steps further along the same path. It does not replace the earlier books: it stands alone yet it also complements *Urban Gardening* very successfully. *Growing Your Own Food in Hong Kong* is another must-have book for every Hong Kong gardener.

In the introduction to Arthur's second book, I asked about a third book. Now it has materialised, another distillation of decades of first-hand experience. Of course I am already clamouring for another book, but in the meantime, enjoy this one: it won't take the hard labour out of gardening, but it will certainly enhance your pleasure and also save you from errors as you go along.

Once again I am honoured and delighted to be able to introduce Arthur's book to all the gardeners and would-be gardeners out there. What a wonderful treasury of knowledge he has produced. Here is your mentor, encyclopaedia, agony uncle all in one.

Jane Ram

Jane Ram is an expert gardener and journalist in Hong Kong. She is a former chairperson of The Hong Kong Gardening Society.

The Scope of this Book

This book is not intended to be a complete gardening manual. There already exists a plethora of gardening texts with detailed information of every aspect of gardening for the beginner as well as the expert. Almost all of these books are published abroad so the information that is correct for Europe or Australia may not apply here. What I hope to provide instead, is information you do not readily find in these books—information specifically for Hong Kong gardeners to succeed in our local conditions. Advice is given that you can actually use, anticipating your questions of what, when, how—what plants to select, when to plant, how to manage a particular problem. Nevertheless, some basic principles and general topics of interest are included for a better understanding of growing your own food in Hong Kong.

I adhere strictly to the principle that only plants that I have personally grown are featured in this book. Since I cannot possibly have grown everything, there are gaps that might disappoint some readers who may find some of their favourites missing.

With the exception of a few photographs of wild plants in their natural habitat, all the photographs were taken in my garden, and all (except for two) were taken by me.

GET GROWING!

"*All that summer, Julian spent her time in the garden with the gardener. She asked him a dozen questions as she watched him pull turnips from the black soil and toss them into a basket. How did he know that the turnips were ready? How did he get them up without breaking the stems? What happened to the turnip if it got too big? Would he plant turnips in the same place next year or somewhere else? He wiped sweat from his forehead and his hands on his mud-spattered tunic. He smiled a deep sun-and-wind-creased smile and laughed heartily at her questions.*"

Amy Frykholm, *Julian of Norwich, a contemplative biography* (2010)

SEEDS AND PROPAGATION

Home-grown food will mostly be started from seeds though some plants are started by vegetative propagation. Seeds vary enormously in size, from the tiny seeds of Chinese spinach to the golf ball stone of the avocado. The seed is probably the most marvellous piece of engineering on the face of the earth. Within its walls is stored nothing less than the blueprint of life itself. Its store of information, its genetic code, exceeds the capacity of any supercomputer. Every time a seed germinates and sheds its carapace, a miracle unfolds as it proceeds to fulfil your expectations, in other words, your "faith" in it. The faith factor is beautifully described in Hebrews 11:1 (King James Version): "*Now faith is the substance of things hoped for, the evidence of things not seen*". A better definition would be hard to find. The seed's blueprint directs the plant's development and behaviour depending on prevailing conditions, and passes information to the plant's cells telling them how they are to grow, what shape or colour each bit of it should be, how they should react to outside attack, how to ensure reproduction and finally how and when they need to pack it in and die.

Saving seeds (chrysanthemum vegetable)

Seeds contain genetic material that will eventually produce replicas of the parent strain. If two strains are crossed, a hybrid results. These are known as F1 hybrids and their seeds produce plants that combine some desirable traits of both parents. The development of hybrids is largely commercially motivated to produce increased yields, uniformity, resistance to pests or diseases, and ease of harvesting. However, F1 plants produce seeds that when grown, do not come true to type and are therefore not suitable for saving. New seeds will have to be purchased every year.

Although the home gardener need not be overly concerned with genetically modified seeds, it is of topical interest and deserves some comment. These transgenic seeds are not produced by hybridisation but by manipulation of genes, that is, inserting favourable genes from an outside source ("genetic engineering") to allow their expression in the modified plant. Like hybrid seeds, farmers who use these seeds are bound to purchase anew from suppliers every year at a much inflated cost. Some see this as a hugely profitable ploy by commercial producers to ensnare farmers into an unequal partnership. The subject of genetically modified, or "GM" food is complex and continues to be hotly debated, especially with many questions about safety still unanswered. For example, will transferring a gene from a peanut also transfer hypersensitivity to peanut protein to the new plant? The debate rages on.

This is an appropriate place to elaborate on heirloom seeds and plants. Heirloom plants are plants that were commonly grown in early periods of human history, but many of which have become underused or even extinct as they give way to the needs of large-scale agriculture. For example, in the 80 years between 1903 and 1983, in the inventory of the National Seed Storage Laboratory in the United States (now the National Center for Genetic Sources Preservation), the number of seed varieties of tomato fell from 408 to 79; cabbage from 544 to 28; peas from 408 to 25; lettuce from 497 to 36 (*National Geographic*, July 2011, p. 117).

Modern farming methods tend to favour only a few varieties which are grown in large monocultural plots to maximise consistency and profits while minimising labour. Whereas this practice has increased yields immensely and has helped to feed a hungry world, it opens up new areas of concern. For example, after the humble potato was introduced to Europe from the Peruvian Andes (where thousands of varieties are still grown), the Irish became dependent on a single, highly productive variety, the Lumper potato. However, its genetic vulnerability to the fungus *Phytophthora infestans* was cruelly exposed in the disastrous Irish potato famine (1845–1852) when the whole country's potato crop failed. This resulted in a million deaths and a haemorrhaging emigration that reduced its population by 25%. Preserving heritage varieties is important in order to maintain a genetic bank to obviate such calamities.

On the Norwegian island of Spitsbergen, the Svalbard Global Seed Vault (the "Doomsday Vault"), half buried in ice fields, was founded in 2006. This facility holds spare copies of seeds collected from gene banks around the world and acts as insurance against the extermination of our future food supply. At present it holds approximately 400,000 seed samples. The storage rooms are kept at -18°C to ensure low metabolic activity and to delay seed ageing. Under these conditions, sorghum seeds, for example, may last 19,000 years. An early advocate of seed collection was the Russian botanist Nikolay Vavilov, who in the 1920s and 30s roamed the world in his quest to collect seeds. He founded an institute now known as the Research Institute of Plant Industry in St. Petersburg. Ironically the man who worked to prevent starvation in the world would himself die of starvation in a gulag in 1943, falling victim to Stalin who considered his seed-collecting a bourgeois activity.

The Slow Food movement is another effort to counter the problems posed by the quick, cheap and easy methods that characterise industrialised agriculture. It was founded in Italy in 1986 by Carlo Petrini to ensure that everyone is entitled to "good, clean and fair food". This is accomplished by striving to maintain biodiversity and therefore a sustainable supply of food. The movement has spread rapidly and has chapters throughout the world, each responsible for preserving the traditional crops and tastes of its own region.

Fortunately, in Southeast Asia many family gardeners and subsistence farmers have never given up heirloom cultivation and the culture of seed saving is well entrenched. Heirloom vegetables have kept their traits through open pollination, producing seeds that can be saved for use the following season. It is therefore a sustainable activity. A growing incentive to re-introduce heirloom culture has gained momentum especially in the last ten years, fuelled by a movement of "locavores" that promotes eating locally-produced food with the unique flavours and properties of heirloom food. Heirloom seeds are now finding a prominent place on the shelves of many seed shops.

Germinating beans

Personally, I engage in seed saving whenever possible. That is not to say that home gardeners should avoid hybrid seeds. Indeed, hybrids perform so well that it is a pleasure to try new ones every year.

Seeds have a limited lifespan, the length depending on conditions of storage. Summers in Hong Kong can do terrible things to seeds, heat and humidity being the worst offenders. Seeds well-kept in cool and dry conditions may last two to three years, but I tend to buy fresh seeds every year if possible. This saves time and frustration. Seeds in Hong Kong are cheap when compared to elsewhere, and investment in a packet of fresh seeds is a wise beginning. Saving money on seeds is false economy. There are exceptions of course: you may have some special seeds that may be difficult to obtain and which you would wish to store for as long as possible. Then again there are seeds from your own plants that you may wish to save for the next season. Seeds should be stored in the lowest shelf of the refrigerator in air-and-water-tight containers. A wine cabinet with an internal temperature of 12–15°C is also a good environment for seed storage and has the added advantage of a lower humidity.

The germination time varies greatly with different plants. Some take two days, while others may take four weeks. In order to know what to expect, some idea of germination times will be provided in the section on individual plants.

There is a reasonably good selection of seeds from various sources in Hong Kong. For local vegetables, there are several shops in Sheung Wan, a few metres west of Western Market that will sell loose seeds that are fresh every year. At the time of writing the minimum purchase would be HK$5–10, which will get you more than you will usually need. Imported packaged seeds are also available at these shops as well as shops in Flower Market Road in Mong Kok. These seeds are sourced from all over the world. Always check the use-by date on the seed packet. However, even this may not be reliable if the shops do not store the seeds properly, which unfortunately is usually the norm rather than the exception. Seeds are also readily available to order by post or online.

A collection of seeds

Seedlings in egg carton

Seedlings before thinning

Seedlings after thinning

SOWING

A general rule is that a seed should be buried as deep as its maximum dimension. A broad bean 2 cm in its main axis should be sown 2 cm deep. For seeds that are very tiny, for example, Chinese spinach, there is no need to bury the seeds at all. Simply scatter the seeds on the soil surface and then gently tamp them into the earth with a flat board or trowel.

The simplest way to sow seeds is to sow them where they are to grow to maturity. Some plants demand this, especially if the seeds are very small, again giving the example of Chinese spinach. These seeds are sown broadcast, that is, not planted individually but collectively, evenly and fairly thickly over the growing area. Other seeds though slightly larger, produce seedlings that are easily damaged by transplanting, for example, carrot. These are best sown directly into the growing site in rows. As the seedlings develop, they will begin to crowd together, at which time they should be thinned by removing the excess seedlings and leaving only those that are to grow to maturity. Large seeds, beans for example, make vigorous early growth so that they too can be sown where they are to grow without suffering transplantation. One needs, however, to take into account the size of the mature plant and to plant the seeds in little holes or "drills" a suitable distance apart from each other.

Many seeds are best started in pots or trays. Sectioned trays are useful and are great space savers. Cardboard egg trays work just as well, though do remember to pierce the bottoms for drainage. There are several advantages here. First, it gives a head start, buying time when space is not yet available in the garden. Second, pots and trays can be moved about depending on conditions—in or out of the sun, out of the wind and heavy rain. The seedlings can be transplanted out when they have become well established and when conditions are right.

Starting seeds in small individual 5–7-cm pots is also a good technique, especially if only a limited number of plants are planned. This would be suitable for medium-sized plants like lettuce, capsicum, cabbage and so on. Sow four seeds in each pot, then select the strongest seedling to grow on and thin out the rest. Transplant when the seedling is showing vigorous growth or when the roots start to crowd the pot or grow out of the drainage holes. Before transplanting, withhold watering so the soil dries out somewhat. This reduces the chances of the root ball disintegrating when it is turned out from the pot. Transplanting in this way is relatively non-traumatic.

Seed tray

Freshly sown seeds should first be kept under cover and out of the sun. As the young plants appear, they should be moved to expose them to increasing light, then full light. This will prevent the seedlings growing tall and skinny from eagerly seeking light—the "rubber-necking" phenomenon. Keep the soil moist and never let seedlings dry out.

Cabbage seedlings in pots ready for planting out

VEGETATIVE PROPAGATION

Soft tip cuttings (Mint)

Soft stem cuttings (Water spinach)

Semi-hardwood cuttings (Matrimony vine)-note the two heel cuttings on the left

Raising plants from seed involves the prior interaction of male and female elements of the plant through pollination. Vegetative propagation, by contrast, is asexual in nature. It can be accomplished by various means such as cuttings, division, layering and offshoots.

Cuttings

Raising plants from cuttings is by far the most widely practised form of vegetative propagation. Part of a living plant—a section of stem, root, leaf or bud—is removed and inserted into a suitable medium and becomes a new plant. An equal mixture of sand and potting soil would be a suitable medium. The cuttings will need light, warmth and moisture before they "take". There should be protection from heavy rain if possible.

Edible fig raised from hardwood cutting after four months

Soft tip or soft stem cuttings are taken from the growing ends or from sections of immature stems respectively, and will be referred to frequently in appropriate parts of the main text. Cuttings should be 9–10 cm long and the stem should include at least two nodes from which new growth will spring forth.

Semi-hardwood cuttings, firmer than soft cuttings, are taken from semi-mature partly woody stems and are useful in the propagation of many shrubs such as matrimony vine. When taking such a cutting from the parent plant, try, if possible, to include a strip of bark from the parent stem. This is known as a "heel" cutting and has a better rate of "take".

Hardwood cuttings afford one of the simplest means of propagation of shrubs and many trees, such as the edible fig. Rooting takes a much longer time than the other forms of cuttings—several months at least.

Division: splitting with a trowel (Chives)

Division

This is the simplest form of vegetative propagation and is used for those clump-forming (e.g. chives) or rhizomatous (e.g. ginger) plants. The plants are simply dug up and split using a trowel or similar implement, and re-planted separately.

Ground layering (Rosemary)

Layering

There are two forms of layering: ground layering and air layering, of which only the simpler ground layering will be discussed. This is a method only suited to those plants with long, low, trailing branches. A wound is created in one of these branches by making a small cut with a sharp knife (taking care not to detach the branch) or bending the branch to produce a crack. The wound is then buried in soil contained in a satellite small plastic pot and the branch held down with a stone or a suitable weight. Rooting should take place in about four weeks after which the new plant can be detached from its mother and raised independently.

Offshoots

Offshoots ready for digging up (Curry leaves)

Some mature plants develop offshoots which spring up close to the base of the parent. These offshoots, although arising from the root system of the mother plant, have already developed a root network of their own, and may be carefully dug up and potted on to grow on their own.

SOIL MANAGEMENT

Owners of newly-built homes with gardens are faced with whatever is left to them by the developer, usually hurriedly deposited soil of poor quality mixed with whatever construction waste he needed to dispose of. This may be topped off with squares of rough turf and hastily transplanted potted plants: an instant garden. Moving into a home with a mature garden will naturally entail less work, but in general the quality of soil in gardens around Hong Kong is very inconsistent. Container gardeners have to make do with what they can scrounge or buy. No matter. The challenge is to work patiently towards the ideal.

Soil is a mixture of mineral particles and organic matter, living and dead, the interstices containing varying amounts of air and water. Some soils, for example clay, consist of very fine particles closely packed together with little space for air and water. These soils are heavy and drain poorly. A sandy soil, on the other hand, is made up of larger particles with more spaces in between. These soils drain rapidly and have poor powers of water retention. Obviously the ideal soil is a happy medium that neither gets waterlogged nor dries out easily. This ideal soil depends for its quality on the right combination of inorganic matter and organic humus. Humus is made up of decomposed animal and vegetable matter and is what gives good soil its dark colour.

Perfect soil or "loam" is light, crumbly, sweet-smelling and a delight to run through your bare hands and fingers. A lean, pale soil that easily dries out should be treated with additions of humus in the form of peatmoss 泥灰土 or compost 堆肥. Peatmoss was once extremely popular, but its excessive use is now frowned upon as the extraction of peatmoss from its natural habitat is considered to be damaging to ecosystems and environmentally destructive. Compost is a much greener alternative and its use should be encouraged. Coir 椰子殼纖維 is increasingly gaining favour as an alternative to peatmoss, although it is not yet freely available. Coir is a natural fibre extracted from coconut husk and is a sustainable resource.

If a soil drains poorly, consider additions of sharp, coarse sand or perlite 白沙. Perlite is a volcanic rock which is mined, crushed and rapidly heated to 1000°C so that it pops like popcorn to result in very light, spongy little granules. In essence it is a lightweight substitute for sand. It improves drainage in a heavy soil and is also a good medium for starting cuttings. Perlite, however, has the annoying habit of floating away during watering, so that a lot of it is lost. You can see how patience is required to achieve a perfect soil!

The more serious or scientifically-minded gardener could consider investing in a soil test kit. All kits come with a set of simple instructions for assessment of the content of nitrogen (N), phosporus (P) and potassium (K—for Kalium), as well as the pH of the soil. The pH can also be simply measured using a pH meter inserted into the soil. pH is expressed on a scale of 1–14. Seven is neutral, any value below this is acidic,

Soil modifiers

any value above is alkaline. Most vegetables like a neutral or slightly acid soil. Ground hydrated limestone 熟石灰, easily and cheaply available from any hardware shop, can be added to correct acidity. Excessive alkalinity can be corrected by acid type fertilisers, peatmoss or sawdust. Liberal watering is also helpful in reducing alkalinity, provided the soil is well drained.

A vertical herb garden

CONTAINERS

The small space gardener will do most of his or her gardening in containers and success will depend on his or her adaptability and versatility. Almost any vegetable can be grown in containers as can many large plants and small trees. Containers allow you to grow many plants you would otherwise not be able to grow for lack of space. Containers can be hung up on walls and fences to open up a new dimension: vertical space. Containers can be moved from outdoors to undercover, from shade to sun and vice versa. This will allow you to escape unfavourable weather conditions and protect your plants.

Practical use of urns

Container gardening is always on the move, testing your ingenuity, never dull. A few fundamentals will help you on your way.

Size and shape

Always select a container of the right size and shape for the intended plant. You will be guided on this point in the section dealing with individual plants. Containers need not only mean flower pots—packing crates, polystyrene boxes, kitchen pots and pans, baskets, barrels, cast-off basins and sinks—anything that holds soil will do. A pot with a width/depth of 12/10 cm of soil is good enough for lettuce, herbs and radishes; 22/20 cm for such plants as cabbage, cauliflower and tomatoes; 27/22 cm for short or medium length carrots, Brussels sprouts and squash. All sizes are approximate. I recommend plastic pots as being the most practical and the easiest to shift about—remember gardening involves a lot of manual labour. Larger plants will need urns which come in many capacities. Most of the urns I use (about 50–70 litres capacity) are obtained free from friendly wet market vendors who happily let me have urns after their contents of bar sugar, pickles, fermented bean curd, etc. have been exhausted. These would otherwise be cast off as garbage. "Thousand-year" black eggs used to be shipped in so-called "dragon urn" (so named for the dragon motif for its external decoration). Unfortunately this supply has dried up as the eggs now come in cardboard boxes. However, these urns are now purpose-produced as flower pots and can be bought at garden centres in varying sizes up to about 150 litres capacity. You may be surprised that I use containers of a smaller size than usually recommended elsewhere—I have found from trial and error that these are sufficient if special care is taken to water and feed.

Soil

In a container, the soil is entirely of your creation. You make up whatever soil you need from whatever is available to you and doctor this, as earlier described, with soil modifiers to produce a porous medium with good drainage yet does not dry out easily.

Watering

Extra attention is needed with containers. They dry out much more readily, especially in hot, dry weather and when the wind is high. If pots are stood on plates, make sure the plants are not waterlogged. Remember to empty the plates after and during a rainy spell. Plants do not like wet feet, but mosquitoes do!

Fertilising

This may need to be done more frequently as much of the nutrients are leached out with watering.

Vegetables in containers

Heat

Summers in Hong Kong can be fatal to pot plants. The high ambient temperature is aggravated by reflected heat from concrete or tile flooring and from surrounding walls. Roof and verandah gardens are particularly vulnerable. Keep pots off the ground by providing "feet" of bricks or tiles. Keep the soil well mulched. A double pot can help provide some insulation.

Re-potting

This becomes necessary when the soil becomes root-bound. Note that some plants enjoy being root-bound. When re-potting, use the next larger size of pot. Cut off any wandering errant roots and shake or scrape off some of the old soil. Score the root ball to encourage new root formation and fill in the gaps with new soil.

Plant selection

You may need to seek out dwarf varieties to suit your container. Tomatoes, sweet corn and many others are available in dwarf form that are particularly suited to container gardening.

To show you what is possible, the photograph on the previous page shows a collection of vegetables—cabbage, Brussels sprouts, lettuce, celery, lemongrass, potatoes, various herbs—all grown in containers. Note the pots hanging on the fence, making use of vertical space.

ORGANIC GARDENING AND FERTILISERS

Organic gardening is essentially a revival of methods that pre-dated the introduction of agriculture and farming systems dependent on chemicals. Organic principles avoid the use of chemically-synthesised fertilisers, pesticides, growth regulators and additives. Instead, reliance is placed on crop rotation, compost and animal manures. Mechanical cultivation of the soil is used to increase productivity, control weeds and pests. Organic farming is intended to be sustainable indefinitely.

Organic production of vegetables is well established within Europe and North America and is rapidly gaining popularity all over the world including Hong Kong. This is largely due to consumer demand for safe food in spite of the higher cost. Local amateur gardeners are taking up the cause, encouraged by such organisations as the Leisure and Cultural Services Department and the Kadoorie Farm and Botanic Gardens. Many first-time gardeners are renting small plots of land in the New Territories and housing estates to start their engagement with the soil. Non-governmental agencies such as the Sustainable Ecological Ethical Development Foundation (SEED) are actively campaigning for more involvement of the urban population. Joining an organic gardening course or becoming a member of a gardening group is a good way forward.

It is interesting to note that until 1978 Hong Kong was largely self-sufficient in vegetables. Since then, farmland in Hong Kong has shrunk alarmingly, falling victim to insatiable developers. At present, according to the Vegetable Marketing Organisation, only 0.13% of our land area is under cultivation, sufficient to produce a mere 2% of our needs. This frightening statistic has led to a call to protect our farms from further erosion to provide food security in a crisis (*South China Morning Post*, May 2, 2011).

I favour organic growing methods, but I am not a slave to it. I try to adhere to the organic ideal but I may succumb if I am faced with an infestation of snails and slugs, in which case I would lay down a minimum amount of snail pellets. But that would be the extent of it. I never ever use chemical pesticides, fertilisers or weedkillers, and my vegetables can be safely consumed on site in the garden itself with a simple swish of water to rinse off the dust.

Perfect soil does not remain perfect. Nutrients are constantly being extracted from it by growing plants or washed away by leaching. Which is why it needs to be managed continually by the addition of fertilisers. I do not use chemical fertilisers, confining myself to organic choices. I am enthusiastic about compost, producing as much as I can and using it freely. Compost breaks down as it works into the soil and has to be replenished from time to time. You can never use too much compost, the greatest value of which is in conditioning the soil. However, since the actual content of nutrients in compost is quite modest, other forms of feeding are required to complement it.

Fertiliser is graded by what is known as its "NPK" value: N for nitrogen, P for phosphate and K for potassium (or Kalium). This should be displayed on the packaging. A fertiliser with a good spread over the NPK range is known as a "complete" fertiliser. As a general rule, high N fertilisers feed leafy plants, while high P and K values are needed for healthy root growth, flowers and fruit. Read the labels carefully before making your purchase.

A favourite local fertiliser is peanut meal or cake 花生麩, the granular residue that is left behind after oil has been pressed from the peanuts. Peanut cake is used by local traditional gardeners and farmers as a sort of universal fertiliser. Its NPK is said to be 3.6:0.7:0.45. I find it particularly effective for leafy vegetables. To avoid attracting ants, mix the peanut cake with an equal volume of soil before laying it down. This will also help to ameliorate the malodour of fermenting peanut cake.

The classic organic fertiliser is manure. Raw manure is difficult to obtain, is messy to use, contains a lot of weed seeds, and contrary to popular belief, has only a modest NPK of about 1:1:1. I rarely use it unless it is given to me by friends who collect it either from stables or from the field. Fresh manure will burn plants and needs to be laid out to age until completely dry before being used. Commercially produced processed manure is a better bet—clean, convenient to handle and to use, though some types are smelly when wet. Organic fertiliser can be prepared from all sorts of animal parts—bones, horns, fur, blood. Plant sources include peanut meal and cottonseed meal. Look around before you decide what to buy. For a liquid organic feed I favour fish oil or urine diluted 10:1. This latter is particularly useful for leafy vegetables as urine has a very high N value. Its NPK value is said to be about 18:4:5.

Organic gardening was taken several steps further by Masanobu Fukuoka of Japan, who, in his 1975 book *A One-Straw Revolution*, played havoc with the well dug-in Japanese agriculture establishment. In the strongest terms he advocated "do nothing farming" or "natural farming" in which he left everything to Nature and eschewed such sacred tasks as ploughing (and even shallow tilling), weeding and fertilising. He argued that natural woodlands and forests have existed and thrived for thousands of years without any human interference and farming should follow this example.

Scathing attacks were made on modern industrial farming methods which ignore Nature's natural rhythm. In these methods Nature is deconstructed and put together again in ways thought to be wise by scientists—elimination of pests, use of fertilisers, monoculture and so on. Hydroponics is an extreme example of human super-control.

Fukuoka's methods have been ridiculed and his efforts widely seen as a quixotic tilting at windmills. But he is vindicated by the outcome: his production per unit area matches or exceeds the most modern Japanese farms. He remained a thorn in the side of the establishment until his death in 2008 at the age of 95. His book is indeed an eye opener as the arguments come from a man who began his career as a scientist and plant pathologist but later experienced an epiphany that changed his life. Reading his book reveals him to be a thought provoking philosopher, even if I am not entirely in agreement with him.

Organic vs. Non-organic

In the end, is home-grown organic food worth the trouble? Some conventionally grown crops may grow faster and larger than organically grown specimens, and may be more pleasing in appearance. The classic example of organic vegetables with holes in their leaves is well known to all. Subjectively, the taste conscious consumer would certainly be hard pressed to detect a difference, whichever way the produce was grown. My original advocacy for organic methods was, in the main, related to the absence of pesticides and other chemical residues and I was not aware of any clinical or epidemiological evidence to recommend organic produce on the basis of content or nutritional value.

My thinking has changed. In a paper published in the *British Journal of Nutrition* in June 2014, a meta-analysis of 343 peer-reviewed articles found that there were highly meaningful differences between organic and non-organically grown crops. The studies showed significantly higher concentrations of antioxidants such as polyphenols in organic vegetables. These antioxidants have been shown in earlier research to be important in reducing the incidence of neurodegenerative, cardiovascular, and various other chronic diseases. In addition, the concentration of pesticide residues was found to be four to five times higher in conventionally grown crops in which much higher levels of the toxic heavy metal cadmium was also detected. The reason for these differences is said to be due to the avoidance of mineral-based nitrogen and phosphate fertilisers that are used to grow conventional vegetables.

In conclusion, the answer to the above question is a clear "yes". Furthermore, it is so gratifying to harvest your food fresh in your own home—and no food miles!

COMPOST

One of the most satisfying things about gardening is making your own compost. Mention compost and I am on my hobby horse. Indeed, it is the cornerstone of organic gardening and provides you with soil conditioner, fertiliser and mulch all at once.

Compost is created from waste organic matter which is collected together and allowed to decompose naturally. A compost heap is a complex and dynamic ecological world of micro-organisms, bacteria, protists, worms, insects, arthropods, maggots and other small animals that break down organic matter, release nutrients and create humus. It would seem that for every type of organic compound there is some specific organism or enzyme system to break it down. The droppings of these small creatures contribute further to the enrichment of the final product. A good deal of heat is generated at the centre of the compost heap indicating that an active biological process is taking place. On a cold winter's morning you may actually see it steaming. This heat, sometimes reaching 55–65°C, will help to kill weed seeds, pathogens, as well as any seeds that happen to germinate. Do not let the temperature go beyond this range as excessive heat will kill off the compost-making organisms as well. Cool the heap down by turning it over with a fork to aerate it. A well-managed compost heap should be clean and odourless.

Compost making is a wonderful way of recycling what would otherwise become trash and to transform it into something that can be returned to the earth that once produced it. Compost making brings about a "feel-good" factor about preserving our environment by reducing our dependency on fertilisers and sparing our landfills. It is just amazing how much waste matter can be swallowed up in a compost maker, thus providing great practical benefits in rubbish disposal. The compost bin, completely full today, will by tomorrow have subsided enough to accept another good load.

The simplest way to start your compost venture is to acquire a purpose-made compost bin which is about the size of a small refrigerator. These bins are made of heavy, black (black colour helps to pull in the sun's heat) plastic material with numerous air vents on the sides. Garden waste is fed in at the top. The compost is removed from the bottom of the pile through a sliding door. Note that only easily decomposable material such as leaves and soft stems should be used. Tea leaves, coffee grounds, potato peelings, pets' fur, hair and natural fibres (wool, cotton) are all

Tumbler type

Compost bin, top loader

welcome. Shredding or cutting the incoming material into small pieces helps to hasten decomposition. Good compost should contain about equal amounts of so-called "green matter" and "brown matter".

Green matter such as fresh leaves, grass cuttings or cabbage leaves have a high nitrogen content and will decompose more rapidly. However, an excess of green matter may result in wet, mushy compost. This should be counterbalanced by adding **brown matter**, rich in carbon, such as straw, paper, shredded cardboard, wood ash, pine needles, dried leaves or sawdust. This soaks up the water, gives body to the compost, and slows down the biological process a little. If on the other hand the compost appears too dry, this is easily rectified by watering.

Leaf mould is another preparation similar to compost. Dry leaves of trees or shrubs may be too acidic, high in carbon and low in nitrogen content for satisfactory bacterial decomposition. Therefore, do not add large quantities of these leaves into your compost heap—this would seriously delay the composting process. Instead collect them to prepare leaf mould which depends on fungal action for decomposition. This takes a lot longer than for ordinary compost, perhaps six months to a year. Pile the leaves together in a large plastic bag and keep them moist to wet. The final product has a very fine, crumbly, brown-black texture with a smell reminiscent of old-growth woodland. Leaf mould is a soil conditioner par excellence, even better than conventional compost, but being low in nitrogen, it provides little in the way of nutrients.

Be aware that the compost heap is not a scrap heap—no kitty litter, rags, disposable nappies, plastic packaging or similar junk please. Avoid glossy magazine paper and coloured ink. Food scraps such as meat, bread, cake, biscuits and dairy products should be avoided so as not to attract vermin.

The addition of a thin layer of soil from time to time will help to introduce more micro-organisms to bolster the biological orchestra. There are proprietary compost activators that inject still larger doses of micro-organisms but I have never found it necessary to use them. Urine, diluted 10:1 can also be used as an activator due to its high nitrogen content. Turning the heap occasionally will help the circulation of air which provides oxygen to hasten the breakdown. As the contents disintegrate, the compost settles to the bottom from where it can be extracted as required after about three months. Once you have got the pile going there is virtually a continuous supply.

The final product should be dry and crumbly, and gives out a sweet, earthy smell. You should be able to plunge your hands into your compost, pull them out and simply dust them clean. Well, that is the ideal, anyway. If your final product does not reach this benchmark, do not despair. Like so many activities, for example baking a cake, there is a certain amount of art to it. Practice and perseverance will eventually carry the day!

Compost can be deployed in two ways: dug in and mixed well with the soil at planting time or as a top dressing for established plants.

Unfortunately compost makers are not easy to find in Hong Kong and my own bin was bought in Canada. They are available at any good garden centre in Europe, North America or Australia. Being of knock-down construction it is easy to bring back as checked baggage. If you are not planning a trip abroad, surf the Net and you will find a number of suppliers for on-line sales. But it is not even necessary to use a commercial product: use your ingenuity and make your own using large rubbish bins. Make holes in the sides for aeration and cut an opening at the base to extract the compost. Yet another and even simpler method is simply to make a round enclosure of heavy wire netting, about 1 m high and use this as a collection point. A brick enclosure will also work. The disadvantage of these simple arrangements is that it will be difficult to insulate the heap against heat loss and the process of decomposition will take a longer time. Attempt some form of insulation by covering with cardboard sheeting or a tarpaulin.

The above method of compost making is known as the static method which is my preferred method. It allows small amounts of waste to be added to the top of the heap at any time and produces compost that can be extracted from the bottom in small amounts for use at frequent intervals. A second method uses tumbler compost bins which consist of a horizontally laid drum that can be rotated with a handle from time to time. By providing better aeration, these bins work a lot faster, but to work best, they need to be filled all at once. The small-time home gardener in Hong Kong will find it impossible to accumulate enough fodder to feed the bin in a short time. Most of these bins are too large for local gardeners although I have seen some mini-bins advertised. These may be worth investigating.

Mention should be made of the concept of "effective microorganisms" (EM) developed by Teruo Higa of Okinawa. This is composed of a heterogenous group of largely anaerobic bacteria purported to promote "friendly" biologic activity in many areas including soil management. It is said to increase the natural resistance of plants to disease and to promote healthy growth by enriching the soil. EM in powder form can be added to a conventional compost heap to speed up the decomposition process but it is mainly used in an intensive composting process known as "Bokashi", invented and marketed by Higa. This has been vigorously promoted among home gardeners to compost kitchen waste to produce a fertiliser in a matter of a few weeks. The principle of EM remains controversial and there are many sceptics. I have not used it myself, largely because there are many gardeners I know who, after an initial spurt of enthusiasm, have given it up as being too troublesome and not meeting expectations.

Green (left) and brown matter

PESTS

Fruit flies trapped by flypaper

What then to do about pests? Simple methods are available. Inspect your plants regularly and pick off the larger pests such as caterpillars. Pesky fruit flies that needle your squashes can be dealt with using sticky flypaper. Aphids and ants are best washed away with a spray of water with or without the addition of soap or detergent. Pests such as mealy bugs and scale can be firmly wiped off with a cotton-gloved hand or scraped off with a spatula or toothbrush. Home-concocted pesticide sprays can be prepared using any form of irritant—vinegar, chilli, garlic and so on. These sprays vary in their effectiveness and are unfortunately very short acting. But keep experimenting with your "jungle juice" and compare notes with your friends.

Various organic sprays and dusts are available commercially, many of doubtful value. One of the better and more widely used ones is neem oil, extracted from the neem tree. This is safe, convenient to use and easily obtainable. I find this moderately effective, but again, short acting.

Natural methods for pest control include biologic agents: beneficial agents—such as the ladybird or the praying mantis against aphids—are increasingly being used not only by large concerns but by backyard growers. Other beneficial insects are lacewings, ground beetles and parasitic wasps.

Interplanting is yet another method to ward off bugs. This involves planting different plants in juxtaposition. Some plants, especially those with strong fragrances such as parsley, rosemary and coriander attract beneficial insects. Colourful flowers planted among vegetables will attract pollinators such as bees. Others such as marigold or nasturtium repel harmful insects and deter nematodes. Examples: plant basil among tomatoes, garlic among cabbages and French marigolds among eggplants.

Seedlings in protective cage

Bird deterrent

"Trap" methods such as the laying down of cabbage leaves or small containers of beer to attract snails and slugs are also frequently used. Scent traps using perforated plastic bottles containing pheromones or highly aromatic fruit juices such as guava juice can attract insects into the bottle and drown them. One problem with this method is that it may attract more than just the local insects. Your trap may attract insects in numbers from far and wide, thus making the problem even worse. There are probably as many tricks as there are gardeners, but most of these techniques are based on anecdote or informal observation: success for some may mean failure for others.

Seedlings are always attractive to birds. A lot of hard work can be wiped out in a matter of minutes by one or two marauding birds. Some protection may be needed in the form of wire netting or cages (cages for cats such as are available in pet shops are useful). Birds ignore scarecrows and are only sometimes wary of whirling pinwheels, but they can be scared off by stringing some discarded compact discs over your crop. The movement, and more importantly, the reflected light from the discs are what keep them away. Some gardeners swear that laying down rubber snakes is a good deterrent, but an equal number will say it is useless! Devices that create noise, such as wind chimes may help.

Look out for signs that warn you of a danger from pests—holes in leaves, droppings of caterpillars, ragged leave edges, mucus trails of snails and slugs.

At the end of the day, it should be remembered that in any activity, gardening included, there is give as well as take. If all caterpillars are destroyed and if all birds are kept away—what kind of a garden would it be without butterflies or birds?

Holes in leaves

Worm and droppings

Bird-damaged leaves

GARDEN MAINTENANCE

Soil management and the role of compost and fertilisers have already been dealt with. But the most important chore would be watering. In parts of the world where wet weather prevails, watering may not be needed for weeks at a time. But in Hong Kong it is practically a daily task. The most common question asked is: how much to water? There is no one answer, but some general principles apply. Watering should not simply moisten the surface soil but should be thorough. Better to water thoroughly and occasionally than lightly and often. But do not be a slave to habit. Test—feel the soil—before you decide whether or not to water. If possible, water directly onto the soil because overhead watering encourages the spread of infective disease. Note also that plants in their dormant phases, for example asparagus in winter, will need little or no water.

More things grow in the garden than what you sow. Which is why the next task is weeding, an essential part of good maintenance. An author of a gardening manual wrote: "*No one in full command of his senses would probably ever feel that weeding is fun.*" By this reckoning I must conclude that I am mentally unhinged. Unhinged I may be but it is weeding that provides me with the therapy I need! Weeding as a quiet and solitary activity leads to an inner calm that no pill or therapist can provide. A dissociation from outside problems and responsibilities is probably what that author, poor fellow, mistook to mean "not being in full command of his senses". Granted the heavy stuff—clearing brambles, long-neglected underbrush and so on—can be a little trying, but like most tasks or scenarios that are considered unpleasant, it is very much a matter of mindset. I like weeding—I only wish I had more time for it. Some weeds are actually very pretty and some are good to eat. I would leave them alone if they are not causing any trouble. The question of propriety is very much dependent on an honest dialogue between weed and man. Weeds also seem to have some kind of intelligence in choosing to grow around plants with which they share some resemblance. Employing camouflage they hope to dupe the gardener in the hope of surviving unnoticed.

Spot the weed among the carrots

THE SEASONS

Wind burn

In Hong Kong we are able to grow things 365 days a year. That is why, whatever the season, it is always the season! Needless to say, seasons must be given their due respect and planting out of time is one of the most frequent mistakes made by the home gardener. Provided you choose the correct plant, every day is a growing day. Broadly speaking food plants can be divided into cool or warm weather crops.

Winter is the prime time for vegetable gardening. The mild temperatures we enjoy will support a huge variety of choices. Temperatures seldom fall below 8°C and even then, only for a few days at a time. Have you noticed that our winters are actually becoming warmer? A change in the weather used to occur in early September but is now not really noticeable until late September or early October. This is the time to plant cool weather crops. A rule of thumb is to plant only when the night time temperature does not exceed 25°C. The main dangers in winter are twofold: dehydration and wind damage. Our winters are dry, which means extra attention needs to be given to keeping plants adequately watered, especially pot-grown plants as they are particularly vulnerable. The north-east monsoon which coincides with the fall in temperature is a fresh, dry wind. It is sometimes very strong, with the potential to cause considerable damage by sucking water out of the soil, and wind burn desiccates foliage. It is difficult to fight this except to keep your pot-grown plants well watered and to remove them to shelter when wind threatens.

Summer can be a difficult time for both plants and the gardener. Mid-summers are swelteringly hot and humid and not conducive to comfortable work outdoors. Fewer vegetables are suited to hot weather and again the proper choice of plant is of paramount importance. March or April is the time to start, making sure the night time temperature does not fall below 20°C. Take your cue from the traditional Ching Ming Festival as the time to sow your summer vegetables. Another tip: by the time you hear the call of the visiting Indian cuckoo (*Cuculus micropterus*), you should have sown your stuff. Its four-note call, on the wing ("mi-rae-mi-doh"), is distinctive. This was

Winter bounty

described in 1951 by the Hong Kong naturalist G.A.C. Herklots as sounding like "one-more-bo-ttle". However, long before Herklots came on the scene, Chinese farmers had for centuries understood this call to mean 早插早熟, in other words, "sow early, reap early": Nature's own message to anyone willing to listen. How much more meaningful and enchanting than "one-more-bo-ttle".

Summer brings danger from torrential tropical rains which can flatten plants and wash away seedlings in no time at all. Rainless days can be just as trying as the hot sun bakes the ground and extracts all moisture from the soil. Pot-grown plants are again most at risk and one might need to move them to shaded areas in the mid-afternoon. But of course, the worst problem in the summers is the tropical cyclone, an average of six reaching these shores every season. The approach of a tropical storm or typhoon necessitates frenzied activity in taking plants to shelter, securing loose objects, and ensuring all drains are working. Picking up the pieces and restoring order after the event is tedious work.

The following list will guide you to select a correct selection of plants for the appropriate season. For greater detail, consult the Planting and Harvest Timeline at the back of the book.

Cool Season

Basil, beetroot, broad beans, broccoli, Brussels sprouts, cabbage, capsicum, carrot, cauliflower, Chinese cabbage, choi sum, chrysanthemum vegetable, cichoria, eggplant, green peas, herbs (various), kai choi, kai lan, kohl rabi, leek, lettuce, matrimony vine, parsnip, pea shoots, potato, radish, snow peas, spinach, sugar peas, sweet corn, sweet potato, Swiss chard, tomato, turnip (including swede and rutabaga), vegetable marrow, white radish.

Warm Season

Asparagus, basil, beans (various), capsicum, Ceylon spinach, Chinese spinach, choi sum (summer variety), cucumber, eggplant, fu muk choi, hairy gourd, kai choi, okra, peanut, squash (various including pumpkin), sweet corn, sweet potato, vegetable marrow, winter melon.

Summer bounty

REASONS FOR FAILURE

The learning process is long and strewn with examples of failure. For harmony to prevail we must work within natural parameters and not be in conflict with them. Any setback should be written into the book of experience thereby turning it into something positive. Thoreau said: *"I have been here these forty years learning the language of these fields that I may better express myself."*

Planting out of season

Don't expect plants to do well out of season—this would be fighting with Nature. If you see vegetables on sale that are out of season they probably come from other parts of the world or from growers who are able to provide micro-climates for their produce—heating, cooling, shading, extra light and so on.

Wrong choice of plants

Be sure not to plant whatever is not suited to our climate. Our warm winters will not support vegetables that need a period of chilling.

Using old or incorrectly stored seeds

Always invest in good, fresh seeds.

Too much shade

Most vegetables would like full sun or at least four hours a day of it.

Too much sun

Especially in the summer, plants can cook in the sun. This applies particularly to rooftop gardeners. Masonry and tiles both absorb and reflect heat. The thermometer shown in the photograph was placed in the summer sun and went beyond the upper register of 50°C and would probably reach 80°C if allowed to do so. Design your rooftop with some shade in mind.

Too much water

Often a problem with containers standing on drip plates which may flood and remain unattended. Especially after rains. This also encourages the breeding of mosquitoes.

Dehydration

Winter winds, summer sun. Water as required or provide some protection. Make sure your soil has abundant humus to retain water.

Alternating dehydration and a surfeit of water

Common with forgetful gardeners who tend to overcompensate when they realise they have neglected their watering duties. This causes such problems as split carrot roots and blossom end rot in tomatoes.

Lack of pest control

Considerable damage can also be done by cats and hungry birds. Fortunately we have no rabbits or moles, but in the New Territories wild boars can be very destructive. There have also been reports of porcupines on the Peak!

Cat's cradle: Smokey the cat in a bed of celery

Allowing disease to spread

Identify plants that have become infected with bacteria or viruses, remove and destroy them promptly. Avoid overhead watering which is a very efficient way to spread pathogens.

Neglecting surface soil maintenance

Get rid of weeds, cultivate around plants to prevent a soil "hard-pan". Top dress with compost.

THE PLANT KINGDOM

TAXONOMY

The practice of gardening does not require any intricate knowledge of the scientific names of plants. The *enjoyment* of gardening, however, is much enhanced by some familiarity with taxonomy, or how plants receive their names. It is, at any rate, an interesting story.

In ancient times living things were simply either animals or plants. Present day taxonomy, or the science of classification, divides living things into five kingdoms: Animalia, Plantae, Fungi, Protista and Monera (or Prokaryota). Our subject, the kingdom **Plantae**, is further sub-divided, in a descending hierarchy, into phylum, class, order, family, genus and species. For everyday purposes we need only concern ourselves with the last three or even just the last two.

Plants are more readily called by their common names as being easier on the tongue. Few would say "*Daucus carota*" instead of "carrot". The problem with common names is that one name may be shared by many completely unrelated plants, for example the name "spinach" can be applied to a number of quite different vegetables. Also, a single plant may have a dozen common names. The matter becomes even more confusing when you factor in different countries, languages and cultures.

Positive identification of a plant only came about when a comprehensive and ground-breaking classification was devised by the Swedish naturalist Carolus Linnaeus (1707–1778). He was born Carl Linné, but for some reason had his name latinised to Carolus Linnaeus. The family name Linnaeus was adopted after a giant linden tree in the family estate. Linnaeus's youth was so unpromising that his father planned a career as a cobbler for him. Fortunately he pulled his socks up and went on to greater things. He studied medicine at Lund and Uppsala, but his greatest contribution was to the natural world. No one was more convinced of his genius than Linnaeus himself. He styled himself "*Princeps Botanicorum*", or "Prince of Botanists" and claimed that his classification was "the greatest achievement in the history of science". It must be admitted that this claim had a good deal of truth to it. Goethe, for example, declared that apart from Shakespeare and Spinoza, no other human being had a greater influence on him.

Before Linnaeus, scientists tied themselves in knots by using elaborate Latin names that could be twenty words long and yet might be altered at will by anybody else. Linnaeus put a stop to that. As a result of his work, a plant's name begins with its **genus,** much like a surname. Within the genus are a number of individual **species** the name of which is written after the genus name. For example *Aesculus pavia* belongs to the genus *Aesculus* and the species *pavia.* Note they are written in italics. The species name is often an indication of the plant's properties: for example, *esculentus* means edible; *oleraceus,* cultivated; *rubra,* red; and so on. This combination of genus and species is known as a **binomial.** This stroke of genius cut through the Gordian knot and was soon adopted by taxonomists as the standard. The first edition of his great work *Systema Naturae* appeared in 1735, a mere 14 pages. By the twelfth edition it had expanded to 2,300 pages.

A collection of several related genera make up a **family**. Growing in the wild or in the garden, a species may, over time, develop some differences in colour or form while retaining the general characteristics of the species. These modified forms are known as **varieties (varietas)**. The variety name follows the species name, for example, *Aesculus pavi humilis,* or *Aesculus pavi* var. *humilus.* A **subspecies** is a natural variant of the species still in the process of evolving and is indicated by "subsp." in ordinary type followed by the epithet in italics, for example, *Beta vulgaris* subsp. *cicla.*

A **synonym** is a recognised name that has been superseded by another. For example, okra is now *Abelmoschus esculentus*, whereas it was *Hibiscus esculentus* previously, which has now become its synonym.

Some varieties which arise not in the wild, but as a result of manipulation during cultivation, are known as **cultivars.** The name of the cultivar is written in ordinary type within single quotations as in *Aesculus hippocastinum* 'Baumannii', often incorporating the name of its originator, in this case Baumann.

Crossing two species belonging to the same genus results in a **hybrid,** which exhibits some traits of both species. A hybrid is given a Latin name prefixed by an "x" sign, as in *Aesculus* x *carnea.* An F1 hybrid is a first generation cross between two strains. An F2 hybrid is a second generation cross between two F1 hybrids.

It is also possible to cross two different but related genera, in which case the "x" sign precedes the name as in x *Cupressocyparis*, a hybrid between the genera *Cuppressus* and *Chamaecyparis.*

A GUIDE TO LATIN NAMES

Is Latin a dead language? It may be so in most arenas, but it can still be helpful in the garden. As mentioned above, some insight into the appearance, origin or habit of the plant can be gathered from the Latin name itself, mostly from the species though sometimes also from the genus name. This is not invariably so, but as far as possible, what information that can be gained from the names of the plants mentioned in the main body of the book is entered below:

acutangula – angled or ridged
aegyptiaca – Egyptian
Allium – onion or garlic-like
americana – American or from the Americas
annum/annus – annual
aquatica/aquaticum – water or grown in water
arvensis – growing in cultivated fields
auricula(r) – ear-shaped
basilicum – basil
batatas – Haitian name for sweet potato
Beta – like a beet
capitata – forming a head
carota – carrot
chinense/chinensis/parachinensis/sinense – Chinese or from China
citratus – citrus
comosus – hairy
coronarium – shaped like a crown
crispum – curled
Cucurbita – shaped like a melon or gourd
domestica – domestic
dulce – sweet
edule – edible, of food
esculenta/esculentum/esculentus – good to eat, tasty
foliosum – leafy
frutescens – shrubby
gemmifera – bearing buds
graveolens – strong smelling
hispida – hairy

hypogaea – under the earth
indica – from India
intybus – resembling chicory
italica – Italian
japonica – Japanese
juncea – resembling a rush
koenigii – kingly
lanceolata – pointed like a lance
longa/longum – long
longipinnatus – long leaves
lunatus – crescent-shaped
majorana – marjoram
majus – major
mays – native American name for corn
melo – melon
melongena – like a melon
moschata – musky scent
nobilis – noble
officinalis – of medicinal value
oleracea – for use in the kitchen, for food
orientale – oriental
pekinensis – from Peking
pepo – sun-ripened
porrum – like a leek
rapa – of or about turnips
rubra – red
Saccharum – sugar
sativa/sativum/sativus – cultivated
sesquipedalis – a foot-and-a-half long
spicata – spiked
tricolor – 3 colours
tuberosum – forming a tuber
undatus – wavy
viridis – green
vulgare/vulgaris – common

PLANTS IN DAILY LIFE

PLANTS AND HEALTH

Two thousand years ago Plutarch advised a moderate diet, exercise and restful sleep as a recipe for good health. Nothing has changed. I will leave the exercise and sleep, and simply deal with the "moderate diet", since as a colorectal surgeon this is an important part of my general advice to patients.

Epidemiological observations have revealed a low incidence of large bowel cancer, diabetes and coronary heart disease in parts of Africa. Poverty in these regions means that these populations consume large quantities of dietary fibre of plant origin, for example from maize, and eat very little red meat. Typically these diets are high in unrefined carbohydrates and produce several soft, bulky stools daily. Conversely, affluent societies with a high consumption of red meat and a low consumption of vegetable fibre have a high incidence of constipation as well as of large bowel cancer, diabetes and coronary heart disease. The message is quite clear.

In my daily work, I see a large number of people with a poor bowel habit, mostly in the form of constipation resulting from a low intake of fibre. The current record, on my books, is six weeks without an evacuation. But for many, even a day or two without a bowel motion throws the whole psyche into disarray and may result in long-term psychological problems.

Cancer aside, constipation contributes to other serious conditions such as haemorrhoids and diverticular disease. This latter is a condition whereby pockets of increased pressure within the colon cause little outpouchings to develop where the colon wall is thinnest—much like little blow-outs. This condition was once rare in Chinese, but in the recent three decades, a change in diet to include more western type food has resulted in a sharp rise in its incidence. Furthermore, evidence-based research has confirmed that the consumption of a fibre-rich diet can protect against diverticular disease. Western dietary habits also account for the appearance in Chinese of certain inflammatory bowel diseases such as ulcerative colitis and Crohn's disease. These conditions, now common, were virtually unknown in Hong Kong when I was a medical student in the early sixties.

Be they humble fishermen or ladies in Prada, most people are understandably reluctant to discuss the very private subject of bowel motions. I have myself, over the years, become inured to any such embarrassment, and will cheerfully embark on a frank and open discussion of scatology. I have become quite skilled in breaking the ice over this subject and it is quite professionally satisfying for me when my patients eventually open up on once taboo subjects such as the frequency, size, colour, consistency, shape and odour of their stool, as well as the effort required to cause its evacuation! Inhibitions now cast aside, they may pull out their smartphones and display colour photographs of the subject. The more enterprising may even rummage among their bags and extricate a plastic container of the real McCoy which we would then critically examine while holding our breaths. This would be their first step to recovery.

My best advice is that one should consume one's daily requirement of nutrients and calories by eating mostly foods of plant origin. Red meat consumption should be limited to 500 g per week. In particular, processed meat such as ham and salami should be avoided as far as possible.

Cruciferous vegetables (so named because their four-petalled flowers resemble the shape of a cross) which belong to the *Brassica* group, are known to provide some protection against cancer. Their action is due to substances called isothiocyanates that alter the metabolism of cancer-producing elements (carcinogens). They are also a good source of fibre. The most effective of this group appears to be broccoli.

The rapid proliferation of health food shops and intrusive advertising claiming the value of special supplements for various conditions, shows that in some areas of society, there is a swing in the opposite direction: excessive concern for one's health, often referred to as "health seeking behaviour". The World Cancer Research Fund concluded that one should aim for all nutritional requirements to be met by diet alone and that dietary supplements are not recommended for cancer prevention. ("Food, Nutrition, Physical Activity and the Prevention of Cancer", 2007, p. xx). A cardiologist once described the vitamin industry as the damnedest racket ever perpetrated upon the public.

Similarly, the obsessive consumption of vegetables that may be perceived to have special healthful effects, for example carrots, celery, garlic and so on, should be discouraged. It should be noted that the claims of herbal medicines are routinely and grossly exaggerated with little or no evidence-based studies. They need to be regarded with caution.

It would be hypocritical for me to advise universal vegetarianism, since I myself have not been converted. I admire vegetarians, but have not the motivation or the will power to make the switch. A varied diet of everything in moderation is a sensible rule. Do, however, limit the consumption of energy-dense foods (over 275 kcal/100 g) and sugary drinks, as obesity ... but that's another story! Suffice to quote Falstaff, Shakespeare's corpulent character:

> *"Thou seest I have more flesh than another man and therefore more frailty."*
>
> (Falstaff to Prince Hal)
>
> *Henry IV*, Part 1, Act III.3

PLANTS AND PEOPLE

Two gardeners happening upon each other are much like two dog owners, strangers bumping into each other. They talk "dog", or "garden", proceed to compare notes, and make friends. Many friendships, and I dare say not a few lasting relationships, are canine-assisted or garden-assisted. But a large gathering of gardeners is more like a medical convention—they talk shop all the time. There is a difference. The doctors are all vying to outdo each other, to advance their careers, always with an eye on the main chance. They seek out and ingratiate themselves with famous colleagues, and get puffed up if a leading light addresses them by their first names in everybody's hearing. Gardeners, on the other hand, are not interested in each other's private lives, social importance, net worth or the colour of your blood. Gardeners are a much more egalitarian bunch. The score? Gardeners 1: Doctors 0.

Gardeners are not always bound by social conventions. What a gardener appreciates may not fit the norm. A doctor wishing to express gratitude to a colleague may make him a gift of, say, a bottle of Chateau Palmer, of a decent vintage no doubt. On the other hand, a gift of buffalo manure from a new gardening friend some years ago was the start of a friendship reinforced periodically by further similar gifts. On reflection, it was a fitting and thoughtful present for a colorectal surgeon. Although, like bringing coals to Newcastle, she was bringing ... here I rest.

Gifts do not stop with buffalo manure. Since I am such a compost activist, friends have taken to depositing their coffee grounds, potato peelings and assorted kitchen waste at my doorstep. Bags of swept up leaves from my neighbouring estate somehow find their way to my garden. My cup runneth over.

That is not to say gardeners are particularly sociable. More likely the opposite. Most of us would prefer to sequester ourselves in the garden, a living place of harmony and balance, to do our own thing, seek solace, and indulge our idiosyncrasies. We can freely mutter to ourselves, talk aloud to our charges or engage in various other peculiar activities. Therefore a neutral observer may not unreasonably find us slightly odd.

As my own vegetable garden is just by the roadside, I have no shortage of neutral observers. Some passers-by would walk straight past a glorious display of giant cabbages rubbing shoulders with a prodigious crop of eggplants, sugar cane, sweet corn and green vegetables without so much as a sideways glance. Would we not, in our turn, consider them odd? To be fair, many passers-by would not only turn to look but would stop and even start up a conversation. Some have become regular visitors. Valuable tips on vegetable growing have been passed on to me from wizened folk who were farmers in their youth but now manual workers employed nearby.

As for myself, I am a willing supplier of spare seeds, seedlings, vegetables and herbs. Shortly before this was written, a woman worker who was repairing some holes in the road shyly walked in and asked if she may have a few sprigs of lemongrass. But of course big sister, what special dish are you planning to cook tonight? Cook? I'll use it to wash my hair, it leaves such a lovely scent and did you know it works for headaches as well? You never stop learning! In fact gardeners are never done with learning. Thomas Jefferson felt this way as he said in his old age: "... *although I am an old man, I am a young gardener*".

And now a true story. Working in my garden one day, in my soiled clothes and battered hat—in other words, as far removed as possible from my normal professional attire of starched white coat—I was unaware of an elegant lady who, it seems, had been watching me for some time. She then hailed me and asked if I was "the gardener". Yes madam, was my reply. She said she admired my work, then proceeded to proposition me—though only to hire me as her part-time gardener. Negotiations were still at an early stage when suddenly she let out a shriek, turned a colour to match my beetroots, and blurted out my name. "Aiyah!! You are my husband's doctor!! Aiyah!! Aiyah!"

PLANTS AND KIDS

Neighbour's daughter Camille gathering her dinner

If urban children seem to have little feeling for Mother Earth, surely this is due to the host of modern day distractions. As a result it is difficult for kids to imagine that rice is produced from a type of grass or that potatoes grow buried in the earth. All food is perceived to come, plastic-wrapped, from the supermarket: no wonder so many children refuse to eat their vegetables! Yet, given a little encouragement, most children will take quite naturally to gardening. What child would not delight to see life spring from a tiny seed, a dry bulb or a seemingly dead twig? And when finally something like a tomato or a radish is produced, their sense of wonder and pride is a pleasure to witness. For this product to be good to eat is a bonus. But nothing kills off interest more than early failure, so it is important to choose "easy" plants to begin with.

For a very young child, it would be best to begin with a large seed, say a broad bean or similar. Take a clean, clear glass jam jar and pack it with cotton wool. Fit three or four beans between the glass and the cotton wool, suspending the beans halfway up the jar. Add water and let the beans get to work. Life begins to unfold. Every new day will see new events, as the seeds swell, send out tentative roots, then the first leaves, then more roots and so on. It never fails to thrill an observant child, but be prepared for questions, questions and questions!

After this initiation, the child can move on to other seeds, bulbs or cuttings. Try planting radish seeds. This is one of the most satisfying for kids because of an attractive product and quick results. Then try something else. A neighbour's little girl once came to me for advice about growing a lettuce in a pot for a classroom competition. I coached her through the whole growing process, and guess what? First prize of course! She is not the only one. Over the years many little visitors have come to my garden to pull up carrots, help with the watering, and occasionally (unintentionally) trample my vegetables underfoot. Whether or not they become future gardeners is not up to me, but it has been a pleasure nonetheless.

Plant a few shallot bulbs in a 12-cm pot and wait a few days for the action to start. For the impatient, buy some fresh spring onions and cut off all the green leaves. Plant the fresh bulbs and roots in a pot and something happens almost at once. Guaranteed changes every day. Then move on to cuttings. Buy some water spinach or sweet potato shoots, cut off a piece of stem with a node, stick this in some soil and enjoy the results.

Want more adventure? Try a climbing plant—beans or squash. This can be a combined project for parents and kids: design and build the trellis together, plant seeds and watch things come to life. This is surely a more lasting interest than bloodthirsty video games.

PLANTS AND ART

Gift basket: a moveable feast

Look at a painting of a cabbage and then look at a real one. You will then understand Paul Cezanne's statement:

> *"I have never tried to reproduce Nature; I have represented it."*

And then you will understand Aristotle's statement:

> *"Art takes Nature as its model."*

Growing plants opens your eyes to Nature's art. Growing your own food does not merely mean eating it, but watching it grow and being awakened by the revelations of Nature. It takes only a little imagination to create edible art which can make a beautiful and meaningful gift, or an unusual ornament for the home.

Vegetable bouquet: edible art

A gift of lettuce ready to go

Cicoria (Bianca di Milano) in a cache pot

The Gardener's Guide To Food Plants

As living things, food plants have certain basic requirements. This is summed up well in a Chinese aphorism 天時 · 地利 · 人和 which, loosely translated, states that clement weather, benevolent earth and harmony with the gardener, leads to a happy conclusion.

Food plants need sun. They are happiest in full, open sun, but they can function quite well with four hours of sun a day. This opens up vegetable cultivation to many verandah gardeners.

Food plants need to be fed by the benevolence of the earth. Though seedlings carry a pre-loaded food supply that lasts about two weeks, they need to draw their nutrients from the soil after this period.

Food plants need the understanding of the gardener who provides the water and the feeding and the protection that the plants require.

ASPARAGUS 露筍 | *Asparagus officinalis*

Asparagus is an ancient vegetable native to the Mediterranean regions and Western Asia, and is believed to have origins dating back to before the time of Christ. This much sought-after and aristocratic vegetable is seldom grown in Hong Kong. This is hardly surprising: our winters are relatively warm whereas asparagus needs a winter dormancy period in order to thrive. It also happens to be one of the very few vegetables that are perennial, which means it needs to occupy a permanent position in the garden all year round even though it sits dormant all the winter months. With space at such a premium in Hong Kong, only those with room to spare will attempt to grow asparagus. I am fortunate enough to have a small corner of my garden which is reserved for an asparagus plant that I have kept going for over 20 years. It is likely to carry on for some time as asparagus is known for its longevity.

Asparagus can be grown from seed but will not produce a crop for four years. Starting up with one-year-old "crowns" or "roots" is a much easier option, as one might expect a crop in the second year. The most popular and successful variety is probably "Mary Washington", valued for its long, thick spears. However, I have never seen crowns for sale in Hong Kong: my own plants are sourced from Australia and Canada. Newer F1 hybrids are said to produce heavier crops.

Asparagus

White spears

Because of its extensive root system, asparagus is a poor choice for containers. Asparagus needs full sun and is quite particular about soil requirements: the soil must be loose and sandy, well drained, with lots of good compost to keep it that way. Weeding is also very important, yet one must not cultivate beyond 3 cm of the soil surface in order not to damage the roots.

The spears appear in the spring—pick them young and tender, and eat them right away, even on site! If white spears are desired, one can cut the spears well below the soil surface just as the spears appear. If left uncut, the spears grow into tall graceful ferny stems with innumerable, tiny linear leaves. These bushy, decorative stems are very attractive and are prized by florists for use as fillers in flower arrangements. The whole plant dies down in the winter, to re-awaken with the onset of warm weather in the spring.

Its species name, "*officinalis*" indicates that it has medicinal value. It is a good source of beta-carotene and has been used by native American Indians for kidney, bladder and heart problems. It is also said to be anti-rheumatic, diuretic, a blood purifier, a regulator of menstrual flow and much else, but it has no application in western medicine.

AVOCADO 牛油果 | *Persea americana*

Avocado flowers

There are three main groups of avocado: the Mexican, the Guatemalan and the West Indian. The one that best suits Hong Kong is probably the West Indian variety. It is an evergreen tree though it sheds leaves from time to time throughout the year. Flowers appear in February or March and the fruits appear from July to September. This form of avocado, probably the "Fuerte" cultivar, is pear-shaped, mid-green, smooth-skinned, and relatively large at about 300 g or more. It is quite different from the smaller, purplish-green crinkle-skinned imported avocados, the "Hass" cultivar. Production tends to be cyclical with good and bad years. I have not seen many trees in Hong Kong. This is a pity, because they are easy to grow from seed and the size of the tree, although naturally very large, can be kept manageable by judicious pruning. Fruiting takes about 8–10 years, but grafted trees are used commercially. If planting from seed, first note that the almost round stone is slightly depressed on one side and smooth on the other. When planting, ensure that the round surface is uppermost as the roots will appear from the depression at the other end. An alternative way of starting from seed is to half immerse the stone in water, held in place by several toothpicks driven into the stone

Avocado

Propagation from seed

Table ready

and resting on the rim of a transparent plastic cup. The obvious advantage of this method is that a visual check on developments can be made at any time. Plant the seedling in soil when it is about 5 cm tall and showing signs of steady growth.

I have a tree which I started from a stone obtained many years ago from a friend's garden in Kowloon Tong. This marvellous garden was attached to a fine old house dating from the turn of the last century. Within the garden were two majestic avocado trees each 20 m high bearing hundreds of fruit, most of which simply fell to the ground and rotted. Sadly the trees have met their demise in the name of development, but their progeny lives on in my garden. Note that avocados will not ripen evenly on the tree, probably because of an inhibitor in the fruit stem. They should be picked when they reach their maximum size and will ripen in about a week at room temperature.

Avocado is considered the most nutritious of all fruits, with a fruit oil content second only to the olive. It has an exceptionally high energy yield at 220 kcal per 100 g. The oil content is of the monounsaturated variety, a healthy fat which raises the blood level of high density (good) cholesterol while lowering low density (bad) cholesterol. The skin is said to have antibiotic properties. An extract of the avocado is used in the cosmetic industry to make beautifying skin creams for sale to those who believe in persuasive advertising.

BEANS / PEAS 豆類

Many—but not all—types of beans grow well in Hong Kong, some as summer crops while others do better in the cool weather. Summer crops should be started from March through May, while cool weather crops should be planted from October through December. Climbing varieties will need some sort of support—a trellis, fence, canes and so forth. More and more bush type plants are being introduced which are compact, suitable for containers and requiring no support. Beans are leguminous plants: remember that their roots enrich the soil with nitrogen that is captured in its growing period. When discarding the spent plants, leave the roots in situ to improve the soil.

Broad bean or Fava bean 蠶豆 | *Vicia faba*

This is an ancient vegetable grown as a cool season crop. The seeds are very large and should be sown where they are to grow 25 cm apart. The plant is a vigorous erect bush with thick stems about 60 cm high. The leaves are coarse to the touch, grey-green. White flowers appear clustered in the upper leaf axils. They are self-pollinating and do not depend on an external pollinator. The flowers give way to large hairy pods each containing four or five flattened beans. Harvest when the pods are mature and the beans reach full size.

Broad bean plant

Some people should never eat broad beans. Here is why. Glucose-6-phosophate-dehydrogenase (G6PD) deficiency is the most common congenital human enzyme defect, and 500–600 million people around the world suffer from this condition. It affects 5.5% of the Hong Kong adult population (Chan, T.K. MD thesis, University of Hong Kong, 1983). After eating broad beans, such individuals develop a condition called "favism" (after "fava" beans) which results in haemolytic anaemia (abnormal destruction of red blood cells), a troublesome though rarely fatal condition. Newborn babies in Hong Kong are routinely screened for G6PD deficiency at birth.

French bean 扁豆 | *Phaseolus vulgaris*

This species shows great variation in both pod and bean structure. Some are grown as pulses (haricot, navy beans) and others as green or yellow beans to be eaten whole as vegetables. They are known by many names: French beans, wax beans, snap beans, string beans, stringless beans and so forth.

French beans

Beans should be started in the spring, from March onwards. These plants were originally vines, climbing by twining, but dwarf varieties have been developed which I much prefer for reasons of space. They are also easier to care for, crop heavily, and can be grown in 23-cm pots. This is a highly recommended summer bean.

Lima beans

Soy beans

Lima bean 莱豆 | *Phaseolus lunatus*

It can be grown in the winter or summer, but avoid the two hottest months of the year. The bush varieties are best but some light staking is usually necessary. The beans are quite delicious and resemble small broad beans. They can be eaten fresh or dried. Cultivation is very similar to French beans.

Soy bean 黃豆 | *Glycine max*

On a global scale, the soy bean is a major commercial player. It is the world's biggest grain legume crop, and its uses, legion. Important soy products are soy sauce, soy paste (miso), tofu and soy milk. Processed soy bean is a valuable source of protein which is used as meat and milk substitutes. In medical practice, soy is an important source of energy supply in intravenous and enteral feeding preparations.

For the small-time gardener, it is an interesting plant, simple to grow. A summer crop, it is an erect annual shrub 50 cm high bearing alternate compound leaves and pea-like flowers. Hairy, narrow pods are produced, 4–8 cm long, containing anywhere from two to five slightly oval seeds. Light staking is helpful. My small crop is usually boiled in the pods, then cooled and eaten as a snack.

Snow pea, Mangetout 荷蘭豆 | *Pisum sativum*

This delicious vegetable is easy to cultivate especially against a fence, and a delight to grow in the cool season. Soak the seeds overnight before sowing them where they are to grow in mid-November, or whenever you are sure the daytime temperature does not exceed 26°C. The leaves are pinnate, terminated with branched tendrils by which they climb. The young plants do not climb very efficiently and you may need to help the process by tying the vine to the support at intervals at a very early stage. The pods are slightly curved, light green in colour. Pick the pods young, when the beans are just beginning to show through. You should be able to harvest the beans in about six or seven weeks.

One of the most popular winter season vegetables is the **pea shoot 豆苗** which grows on a plant so closely comparable to the snow pea that it is almost impossible to tell them apart until such time as the pods appear. These pods are thicker and coarser, though still edible when young, but it is the young growing shoots, known as tau miu which are picked and eaten as a vegetable. This is an expensive vegetable to buy in the wet markets because a large number of plants—probably more than you can grow at home—are required to produce even a modest harvest of shoots for a single meal. If you wish to grow pea shoots, make sure to ask very specifically for tau miu seed at the time of purchase.

The **sugar pea** or **snap pea** 糖豆 is very similar, except that the pod itself is fleshy and rather crunchy in texture. The ordinary garden **green pea** 青豆 is another variation, but it is the shelled pea itself that is eaten and not the mature fibrous pods.

Snow peas

Sugar peas

Garden green peas

Pea shoots

String bean, Yard-long bean 豆角 | *Vigna sesquipedalis*

It is without doubt my favourite summer bean. It comes in two forms, a green 青豆角 and a white (actually a light green) 白豆角. The former is more slender, crunchier, generally of superior eating quality and should reach about 35 cm in length. In any case, pick them young when the beans just begin to swell within the pods.

String beans "green"

String beans "white"

It should be started in March to May while the white variety is usually better off a little later, May to August. The white variety is even more prolific, reaching 45 cm or more in length, but it can become fibrous very quickly. These plants climb by twining and a good support is required. Plant three seeds at the base of each support. The seeds germinate in about four days. The sooner the young plants reach support, the faster they grow, so consider tying them early to their supports. Stop the plants as they reach the top of the support. As the light mauve flowers appear, begin to thin out as many leaves as necessary to expose the developing flowers to sufficient sunlight. These thinnings are edible though rather coarse, and are best used to prepare light soup. Thinning should be done quite energetically every four or five days—this is important to remember if a good crop is to result.

Ants and aphids can be a problem, with the ants "shepherding" the aphids along the vine. Physically rub them off with a gloved hand or wash them off with a strong water spray.

A word about **runner beans** which I have tried to grow repeatedly without any success. The plants grow lustily enough and produce their attractive red flowers. However, beans either do not form or appear stunted. Writing in 1913, W.J. Tutcher, Superintendent of the Botanical and Forestry Department of that time, also reported failure in growing runners and felt that "in all probability, there is no insect in the Colony suitable for fertilising the flowers, or if there is, it does not do so".

BEETROOT / SWISS CHARD (Spinach beet)

紅菜頭 / 君達菜 | *Beta vulgaris* subsp. *vulgaris* / *Beta vulgaris* subsp. *cicla*

Beetroot is not a particularly popular vegetable in Hong Kong and is not consistently available in markets. All the more reason to grow your own! They are great eaten raw, cooked or pickled. Borscht owes its rich red colouration to the abundant use of beets. The tops can also be eaten or used in soups.

Beets enjoy a light soil with excellent drainage. Sow the seeds where they are to grow: three of the large spiky seeds in 2 cm deep drills 10 cm apart. Sowing should start in October and in succession through January. A little patience is required as the seeds are usually slow to germinate. This can be speeded up by soaking the seeds in water for a few hours before sowing. As the seedlings grow, thin out to favour the strongest one. Alternatively, simply scatter the seeds closely, then thin out the tiny beets as they begin to crowd each other, when they are about the size of a radish. These thinnings are good to eat or to use in soups. Keep well watered to encourage rapid growth. Any check in growth or change in conditions is likely to lead to bolting. As the plants develop above the ground, cultivate the surrounding soil and heap it against the enlarging globes. Extreme care must be taken not to injure the beets while doing this, to prevent "bleeding". Harvest when they are about the size of a small orange, again taking care not to breach the skin.

Beetroot

Beta v. subsp. *cicla* comprises the leafy vegetables Swiss chard, silver beet and ruby chard. These types are only occasionally seen on sale in supermarkets and are rather costly. Chard can be eaten raw in salads but I much prefer it cooked when it tastes much like spinach. A coarser, all-green variety is commonly available in wet markets and is the only form farmed in Hong Kong. These vegetables have large, luxuriant, shiny, puckered, fleshy leaves with broad, crisp ribs. The waxy stalks may be white, red, orange or yellow, and chard is attractive enough to grow as ornamentals, especially in a mix of colours. You may find them too pretty to harvest and eat! Pick only the outer leaves for use as required, thus prolonging production for months.

They are so easy to grow as a cool weather crop and are of such good eating quality that it is surprising they do not receive more attention commercially. The plants are tall, up to 40 cm, and are heavy feeders. Start from seeds sown where they are to grow in drills at least 25 cm apart. Make the drills at least 5 cm deep while covering the seeds with 1 cm of earth. As the seedlings appear, fill the drills to provide lateral support for the rapidly growing young plants.

Swiss chard

Swiss chard in pots

BROCCOLI 西蘭花 | *Brassica oleracea* var. *italica*

Broccoli is very similar to Chinese flowering kale, or kai lan, both in its early appearance and in its flavour. It can also be considered another variety of cauliflower though with green, smaller heads and fleshy stalks which are also eaten. Some types have purple or yellow-green heads. Sprouting broccoli is a separate variety with a large number of much smaller curds, produced in rapid succession. This variety needs cooler weather, and I have not seen it grown successfully in Hong Kong.

Plant the seeds from October to January, using 5-cm pots, four seeds to a pot. Afterwards keep the strongest of the seedlings and thin out the rest. Plant out when the roots begin to fill the pot, when the seedling is about 5–7 cm high. Each plant needs quite a bit of space, about 25 cm each way. Harvest the heads when the flowers are still closed and compact, just before they show signs of opening, and include about 10 cm of stem and leaves. A small secondary harvest of edible shoots can be expected from the remaining plant.

Broccoli is one of the most nutritious of all vegetables, with a low calorific value, a high protein content of 3%, and a rich supply of vitamins and minerals. There is good evidence that the consumption of cruciferous vegetables can lower the incidence of bowel cancer. Broccoli is a member of this group and is believed to be the most beneficial of all.

Broccoli

BRUSSELS SPROUTS

抱子甘藍

Brassica oleracea var. *gemmifera*

This cool season vegetable can be grown with reasonable results in Hong Kong, though with our winters getting warmer it may be a problem in the future. Sprouts prefer a prolonged period of cold weather. The plants are rather bulky, with an erect stem and a leafy crown. In order to save space, I prefer to grow them individually, one to a large 30-cm pot. Start the seeds much in the same way as cabbage. The sprouts appear as miniature cabbages one to each leaf axil. Remove the lower leaves as they turn yellow. Special attention must be taken with pot-grown plants which need to be well watered and regularly fed every two weeks. When production is exhausted, after about four months, the top of the plant, which now resembles a small cabbage, can be eaten as greens with a flavour very similar to kai lan.

Brussels sprouts

CABBAGE 椰菜 | *Brassica oleracea* var. *capitata*

Cabbage

Pieris rapae, small white butterfly

I grow cabbage every year largely on account of the satisfaction of watching it grow, especially the day-to-day changes as the heads take form. The growing period is rather long, three to four months, but the end product is a pleasure to behold whether grown in rows or in pots.

Brassica is a remarkable genus, providing a greater number of important vegetables than any other. There are so many varieties of cabbage that it is difficult to recommend a particular one. Not all are suitable for our subtropical Hong Kong so one should choose carefully and read the fine print before buying a packet of seed. I have a limited experience of the vast choices available, but twist my arm and I might suggest "Blue Star" or "Full Moon", both F1 hybrids, the former from Japan and the latter from Taiwan. Another interesting cabbage is the Filderkraut cabbage, a German heritage variety with pointed, conical heads. This cabbage is very large with outer leaves double the size of a tennis racquet. The head itself is enormous—shed of its outer leaves, the largest I have grown weighed in at 5.8 kg. Filderkraut is the favoured variety for making sauerkraut.

Although it is best grown in the ground, cabbage can very successfully—and attractively—be grown in 25–30-cm pots provided drainage is good and it is kept well watered. The seeds should be sown, September through November, in small 5–7-cm starting pots, four seeds to each pot. As the seedlings appear (usually within a week), select the strongest and thin out the rest. When the seedlings are about 10 cm high, or when the roots crowd the pot, transplant to its final growing site in the ground 60 cm apart or to a larger pot. Full sun is best.

Cabbage worms, snails and slugs can be a problem, so keep an eagle eye open and pick them off as they are found. Active worms leave their calling cards: droppings around the plants or holes in the leaves. The pest that causes most problems with my cabbages is the small white butterfly (*Pieris rapae*) which in its caterpillar form can wreak havoc in a single day.

As the cabbage grows, the dark green outer leaves can be removed from time to time to open up space, let in light, and to prevent crowding. These leaves need not be discarded as they make a wonderful contribution to any vegetable soup such as the earthy Portuguese soup "Caldo Verde". The heads should be harvested when they form a firm ball, and well before the young leaves show signs of splitting. A cabbage ready

Filderkraut cabbage

for harvesting is beautiful to behold: the light green solid head nestled in the midst of a protective bed of darker outer leaves, all the more striking if planted in a row. A freshly harvested cabbage makes a splendid table centre for a few days, like a work of art.

Collard greens are a loose leaf cultivar of *B. oleracea*. I have never seen them in Hong Kong, where our selection of green leafy vegetables is so varied as to elbow collard greens into insignificance.

Savoy cabbage is a round-headed cabbage with crinkly, strongly-veined leaves giving it a rather "noble" appearance. Slower in growth habit, it thrives in very cold winters but reasonably large heads can still be successfully grown in Hong Kong. They tend to have a stronger flavour than ordinary cabbages and have a novelty value.

Red cabbage is another interesting variety grown mainly for pickling. It too enjoys cold winters but satisfactory results can be obtained in Hong Kong.

Some cabbages are grown for ornamental purposes. They are round-headed cabbages with crinkly leaves variegated in pink, purple and white. They are much valued for flower arrangements and as pot-grown ornamentals.

Savoy cabbage

Red cabbage

CABBAGE, CHINESE 黃芽白 | *Brassica pekinensis*

It is available year-round in our markets, a testament to its excellent keeping qualities. Huge quantities are grown in Northern China, and at harvest time, mountains of piled-up cabbages are stored in barns or left under tarpaulins on roadsides, ready for the severe winter months ahead. Every household would have its own private stockpile. Vegetable vendors often hang the cabbage upside-down and allow it to wilt somewhat. There are people who believe this adds to the sweetness of the vegetable. This may be true, and if so, is most likely because of the lowered water content. I myself cannot detect any difference.

Although it can be eaten raw, I have never actually seen it served in salads. It is much better stir-fried or used in soup. The well-known Korean pickle kimchi is made from this cabbage. It has also an established popularity in western countries.

This cabbage is composed of a densely packed collection of yellowish-green toothed leaves with wide leaf stalks. The cabbage may take an elongated form, sometimes referred to as Tientsin cabbage, or a bulkier, barrel-shaped form usually with paler-coloured leaves. In subtropical Hong Kong, this vegetable grows dependably and rapidly in our winters, and is one of the first cool season vegetables that I plant every year, followed by a second sowing two months later.

Cultivation is no different from cabbage—grow in the ground or in pots, in full sun. When the plants are nearing maturity, it is best to tie up the outer leaves in order to achieve a moderate blanching of the hearts. This, however, presents its own problems, since pests such as caterpillars, aphids and especially snails and slugs may then happily thrive snugly out of sight. Another problem with tying up is the possible trapping of

Chinese cabbage in a pot

Tied up for blanching

Chinese cabbage long form

Barrel-shaped

water between the leaves, leading to rot. It is therefore necessary, from time to time, to release the ties and make a good inspection of the situation. Aphids are particularly prone to appear if the weather is unseasonably warm. The best way to deal with them is to wash them off with a strong spray of water, trying your best of course, not to damage the plant itself. The time to harvest is when the hearts are firm and compact. It would not be unusual to expect a 2–3 kg specimen.

CAPSICUM 辣椒 / 牛角椒 / 燈籠椒 | *Capsicum*

Capsicum is a genus of many small shrubs, annuals or treated as such. Capsicum is thought to have originated in tropical America though it is now freely used to stoke fire in Eastern and Southern Asian cuisines. It would be hard to imagine these cuisines without the heat of the chilli. Indeed, so embedded is the chilli in these cultures that an Indian, a Thai or a Chinese may well swear that the chilli is native to their country. Do not try to tell them that it was most likely Christopher Columbus who brought it back with him from the new world in the 15th century.

Capsicum annum provides the greatest variation in fruit characteristics and is a bewildering collection of peppers of all shapes, colours and sizes, from the familiar bell peppers used in salads to tiny hot chillies. Its diagnostic feature is that the flowers are usually solitary with recurved stalks. A rule of thumb: the smaller the chilli, the hotter it is.

Cultivars form three broad groups. The **Grossum** group includes the main salad peppers, including pimento, bell and sweet peppers. The **Longum** group has fruits that are elongated, often curved, mild to medium-hot peppers. Cayenne, paprika and the banana peppers belong to this group. The **Conoides** group has conical fruits, usually small and very hot. These include some beautifully coloured fruits of varied shapes that are used as ornamental pot plants. Note though that they may easily be confused with similar ornamental solanums whose fruits are actually poisonous.

Long red chilli

Bell pepper

Habanero

Friar's hat

Cone chilli

Green chilli

Some of the capsicums grown locally are *C. frutescens*. These are very hot chillies and can be easily distinguished from *C. annum* by having two or more flowers to each leaf axil whereas the latter produces a single flower. Some of the best-known chillies, such as the 'Tabasco' cultivar and the 'Habanero', belong to this group.

Purple beauty

Recent publicity has been given to what might be the hottest chilli on the planet. The "heat" in the chilli is due to its content of a molecule known as capsaicin, which is thought to be part of the plant's defence mechanism. (I have my doubts as to this function, though, as I have watched, many a time, some birds, especially crested mynahs, devour my chillies in a matter of minutes.)

Giant red cone chilli

We now have a unit for the measurement of a chilli's hotness, known as the Scoville Heat Unit (SHU) named after Wilbur Scoville, a one-time pharmacologist with the Parke-Davis Company. Here's a short league table of the hotness currency of some chilli varieties: A typical hot Thai chilli measures 50–100,000 SHUs, similar to the famous Tabasco cultivar (*C. frutescens* cv. 'Tabasco'). A Scotch bonnet is an innocent-looking orangey-red fruit the size of a chestnut that can measure anywhere from 150–300,000 SHUs. This chilli is so hot that, having tried it, I believe it should come attached to a warning label. Indeed, a knife used to cut the chilli will still sting your tongue the next day even after several washings. Yet I do know nice, delicate ladies who consume it regularly! The red habanero is similar, probably a little hotter at 300–500,000 SHUs. Up to very recently, this was thought to be the absolute limit of hotness. However, in recent years, an obscure chilli known previously only in South Asia has surfaced wearing the yellow jersey. This is the bhut jolokia, also known as the naga or ghost chilli which weighs in at over 1,000,000 SHUs. It is hard to imagine who would ever use it, but believe me folks, some people really do! There is the tale reported in the *Christian Science Monitor* of an Indian woman in the northeastern state of Assam who ate 51 bhut jolokias in the presence of the British chef Gordon Ramsay, apparently remaining alive after her performance. As for me, I would not approach it without a lead-lined suit.

Capsicum frutescens

One does not stay on top of the pile for long. The Naga viper chilli soon displaced the bhut jolokia with a claimed 1,300,000 SHU only to be toppled, a short time later, by the current champion the Trinidad Scorpion at 2,000,000 SHU (Hong Kong Gardening Society Newsletter October/November 2013). It is difficult to imagine how these chillies can be of any practical use in the kitchen.

On a more serious note, capsaicin does have therapeutic value and is now available in special creams and lotions for the relief of pain and inflammation of arthritis, nasal congestion, insect bites and so on. It is said to release beta endorphins in the brain, leading to pain relief and a "high" feeling. Pepper spray used by police to subdue violent or unruly individuals and crowds has capsaicin as its main ingredient.

The plants are small shrubs ranging from 15–80 cm. The leaves are simple and smooth. Plain white flowers are borne in the upper leaf axils. Although usually grown as annuals, if a specimen remains healthy, it may survive and continue producing for another year or two. Capsicums can be grown all year round, although bell peppers do better sown as a cool weather crop in late October. Sow the seeds in little starter pots and transplant into the ground 20 cm apart, or into 25-cm pots. Full sun is best although pot-grown plants may need to be taken out of the worst of the mid-afternoon summer sun as well as needing watering three times a day.

Plants are sometimes infested with red spider mites. If so, try washing them off with a water spray or deploying one of your homemade organic pesticides. What is more challenging is infection with the tobacco mosaic virus. This has been a common problem among my plants. This causes the young leaves to yellow and shrivel up in a fern-like manner. It is a challenge that can only be met by a take-no-prisoners approach—simply destroy the plants as soon as possible and remove them from the vicinity of the garden to prevent the spread of infection.

If you have chillies to spare, consider stringing them up to dry—I always have some hanging in my sitting room for decoration. The dried chillies can then be used a few at a time as required. Chillies may also be preserved in vinegar for later use. Adding them to a bottle of soy sauce gives it a delightful kick. Homemade chilli sauce is yet another option, the recipe of which is in a later section.

CARROT 甘筍 | *Daucus carota*

What is a vegetable garden without carrots? One of the pleasures I get out of growing carrots is for me to invite small children to pull them up. If they have never done this before, it is guaranteed to produce squeals of excited pleasure when the colourful carrot suddenly pops up.

Carrot: Atomic Red

In a good seed shop you may be confused by the many varieties of carrots on offer. Generally they can be divided into short-, medium- or long-rooted. I usually pick a medium-rooted "Nantes" as a reliable performer, although "Chantenay" also does well. Long-rooted carrots are very appealing aesthetically though they need deep, loose, stone-free soil in order to develop properly. One such cultivar is "Atomic Red" which produces richly-coloured, long, tapering roots. F1 hybrids such as "Fly Away" offer advantages such as resistance to carrot flies. Can carrots be grown in pots? Yes, but choose the short- or medium-rooted types with four plants to a 23-cm pot.

Sow the seeds fairly thickly where they are to grow since carrot seedlings do not transplant well. Sow into rows 3 cm deep and 7 cm apart. If this sounds like overcrowding, you are right, but don't worry, I find it works well as carrots do not need as much space

Purple carrot: thinnings for salad

as some believe. Cover the seeds with a thin layer of fine soil, not reaching the brim of the row. The seeds germinate in 7–10 days. As the seedlings become established they may look a little spindly and floppy. Now then is the time to push the soil in from the side to level up the row and firm them up. Thin the seedlings, leaving the remaining seedlings about 3–5 cm apart—that is all the space they need. These thinnings will have formed miniature little carrots useful in salads as shown in the photograph.

Keep the plants well watered and use a liquid feed every two weeks. Irregular watering may result in split roots. In comparison to some root crops such as the white radish, the growing period is quite long, about three or four months, but the wait is worth the trouble. Fortunately carrots remain in good condition long after maturity and so can be harvested at leisure over an extended period of time.

I have had little trouble with pests or diseases but one little point deserves mention. Carrots can be sown from the end of August onwards, but I always wait till October when the threat of heavy rains has passed. All it needs is for one heavy downpour to wipe out seedlings started too early—a lesson I have learnt.

Romanesco broccoli / cauliflower

CAULIFLOWER 椰菜花

Brassica oleracea var. *botrytis*

This is a cool weather vegetable with a history stretching back to the Renaissance. It is grown for its large clusters of thick-stalked, unopened white flowers growing at the centre of a rosette of large, grey-green leaves. Green or purple heads are also known. Another sub-group of cauliflower, which I have recently grown, has clusters of pyramidal-shaped florets, but this is often confused with or classified as broccoli—Romanesco broccoli. The unusual appearance of the florets is regarded as beautiful by some but as grotesque by others who view the florets as reminiscent of unsightly warty growths. You have to judge for yourself!

The cultivation of cauliflower is not difficult, being similar to cabbage, and like cabbage it has a relatively long growing period of three to four months. It is a large plant and should be given adequate space to develop if grown in the ground. Pot culture is possible, using 25–30-cm pots for each plant, although one's expectations in respect of size should be rather more modest.

The soil needs to be humus-rich and continually cultivated around the plant, heaping earth against it from time to time. Water generously and pay special attention to pot-grown plants which are prone to drying out in the sun. Feed every two weeks with a liquid fertiliser or peanut cake which I find very effective for Brassicas. When the curds approach maturity—heads of about 15 cm are normal—you may break the ribs of the surrounding leaves for them to fall over the curds to shield it from most of the sun in order to keep the colour white. The leaves can also be tied with string or secured with an elastic band. Still another method is to place a heavy plate onto the curds. Check for pests regularly. If the curds start to split, show a purplish discolouration, or become a little hairy, you have left harvesting too late. Raw, fresh, young, home-grown cauliflower, free of pesticides, is wonderfully crunchy and a great addition to salads.

Cauliflower

Keeping the curds white

Purple cauliflower

CELERY 西芹/芹菜 | *Apium graveolens*

This popular cool weather vegetable occurs throughout Europe, temperate Asia and the cooler parts of the southern hemisphere. It is grown for its tight cluster of light green, crescent-sectioned stalks or petioles. It is eaten raw in salads, or cooked in Chinese cuisine, in soups, and together with carrots and onions makes up the *mire poix* essential in stews and soups in western cooking.

Start the seeds in the usual way in October and transplant into 25-cm pots or into the ground 20 cm apart. Since it takes about four months to reach maturity, I prefer the pot option in order to save ground space. As it grows, any basal shoots that appear should be rubbed off. Keep well watered at all times. One is sometimes advised to earth up the stalks as they near maturity in order to keep them from turning a darker green. I have never done this and do not find it necessary. Celery prefers a longer, cooler winter than we can offer, but some pretty decent specimens can still be produced at harvest time.

What I do grow on a regular basis is Chinese celery (*Apium graveolens L.* var. *dulce*) 芹菜. The whole plant is much more slender than salad celery with stalks that are very slim and fibrous, not suitable for eating raw. As a cooked vegetable, however, it has a decidedly stronger flavour than salad celery and I find it more effective in stews and soups. It is excellent in a vegetarian stir-fry or paired with other vegetables or fish. The stalks are slender and together with the leaves are about 40 cm tall. As seen in wet markets, the plants are sold whole with the roots.

Sow the seeds fairly thickly directly into the soil or the pot in which it is to grow. This results in a thick bunch of plants that will not grow very tall, but the crowding is a natural way to keep the stalks shielded from the sun and therefore remain a pleasantly

Celery

Chinese celery

pale colour. The plants are thinned out when necessary as they grow. These thinnings can of course be used in the kitchen. Otherwise they need very little care. Rather than pull the plants up whole, I harvest the stalks as they are needed, leaving the plant to continue production. With careful harvesting a single sowing will last all season.

Celery is an ancient vegetable that has been in cultivation for 2,000 years. It was originally a wild plant (in England known as "smallage") which was gathered for medicinal uses. It has high nutritional value including a high protein content. In traditional medicine it has been used for lowering blood pressure as well as for a diverse collection of maladies that is too lengthy to list.

CEYLON SPINACH (Malabar spinach, Climbing spinach)

潺菜 | *Basella rubra L.* var. *alba*

This is not a true spinach, but a glabrous succulent climber whose leaves resemble spinach. It can be used in much the same way although it has not achieved much popularity. As a tropical species, this is a summer crop and a very useful one since it is one of only four leafy green vegetables that can routinely succeed in the blistering Hong Kong summers. The other three are Chinese spinach, water spinach and kai choi.

The leaves are shiny and fleshy which are eaten together with the petioles and young stems. Its main characteristic is that it has a slimy or mucilaginous texture which may not suit all palates. It can be stir-fried, flavoured with sesame oil and chilli, but it is best used to make a simple boiled soup. A cultivar with reddish-purple colouration is also quite common. The plants grow quickly in just about any type of soil. They can be harvested when they reach 10–15 cm tall, cutting with a sharp knife but leaving a 4-cm stump from which new growth will spring up again. If given support and left to grow on, it rapidly becomes a vine that climbs by twining. Simply pick the leaves for use as you need them. One sowing from March through May will keep you supplied for the season. The seeds are best sown directly into the ground. It is also possible to propagate using stem cuttings which grow very easily.

Ceylon spinach is rich in calcium, iron, and vitamins A and C. It has medicinal properties as a mild laxative.

Ceylon spinach

CHAYOTE (Vegetable pear)

合掌瓜 / 佛掌瓜 / 佛手瓜 | *Sechium edule*

This is a strong-growing perennial vine that needs lots of space and may not be suitable for containers in a small garden. It is native to Central America where it may still be found growing in the wild, producing bitter fruit.

Chayote belongs to the gourd family *Cucurbitaceae*, related to the melons, squashes and cucumbers, but the pear-shaped fruit with a single seed is unique. The leaves are heart-shaped and the flowers very small and pale yellow. Grow the vine in late summer by planting the whole fruit with the contained seed and the narrow end slightly exposed. Please note that planting the seed alone will almost certainly result in failure. While quite easy to grow, the difficulty lies in obtaining a sufficiently mature fruit to plant.

An ideal fruit would show the beginnings of a sprouting seed. Most of the marketable fruit are too young to use and some effort is required in searching the markets for a dry, unattractive old specimen—which the vendor will be only too happy to get rid of! Or perhaps try obtaining one from a friend who has an established plant.

Chayote

Chayote seedling arising from the whole fruit

CHINESE SPINACH (Amaranth) 莧菜 | *Amaranthus tricolor*

Chinese spinach

Red-veined Chinese spinach

All-red amaranth

Chinese spinach is one of many cultivated strains of *Amaranthus tricolor* and is the only one used as a leafy vegetable. Most of the other strains, though sharing the same name, are quick growing ornamental annuals used as colourful bedding plants or as showy, short-lived, bushy shrubs. These plants are native to Africa and Asia.

This vegetable is especially important as it is one of the few leafy green vegetables that can be grown reliably in our very hot summers. The leaves are mid-green in colour, rounded or elliptical. A red-leaf version is also grown, although it is only the veins that are red while the rest of the leaf and the stalk are green. It is identical in taste to the green variety, although it "bleeds" when cooked. Not long ago I was given some seeds of yet another variety that is completely red throughout stems and leaves. I am told that an extract from this plant is used as a red dye by the Hopi Indians in western USA, and I suspect it is native to that region.

Seeds of the Chinese spinach are jet black, tiny, shiny and hard. Oddly, the seeds of the all-red variety are completely different, being slightly larger and a pale cream in colour. The seeds should be scattered evenly and fairly thickly where they are to grow, as the seedlings are very delicate and not suitable for transplanting. Either cover the seeds lightly with a thin layer of fine soil or simply press the seeds into the earth with a flat board or trowel. Water gently. Seedlings appear in profusion after three or four days, and frequent thinning will be needed to allow the remaining favoured plants to grow to their full height of about 25 cm. Harvest in about four weeks, before the flowers appear. Chinese spinach is sold in the markets as a complete plant, roots and all. The home gardener can be a little more thrifty: cut the stems, leaving several axillary shoots to provide a second or even a third cutting.

Chinese spinach may be grown in pots: a 25-cm pot will provide a constant supply for three or four weeks. One very important advantage of growing in pots is that the pots can be moved under cover during rainy spells. I have had outdoor sowings washed away by summer rainstorms more times than I care to remember and now tend to use the pot option more often.

I enjoy this vegetable best lightly cooked with lashings of chopped garlic. I have seen it served in salads, but in my opinion it doesn't taste quite right in the raw state. Chinese spinach is very high in nutritional value being especially rich in iron.

CHOI SUM (Chinese flowering cabbage) 菜心

Brassica parachinensis

Chinese flowering cabbage is arguably the most popular local leafy vegetable, a title contested only by pak choi. It is a winter crop although a summer variant is available. This, however, is of lower eating quality. The leaves are elliptic, strongly venose, mid-green in colour, about six to eight leaves to each plant. The stem is light green, reaching a height of 20–25 cm. The flowering spike is also eaten, and in my opinion, is the most delicious part of the plant. Strangely, in Chinese restaurants, the flowering spike is often removed before serving. I have not received a satisfactory explanation as to why this is so.

Seeds are classified according to the time taken to reach maturity: 30, 40, 50, 60, 70 or even 80 days. As a general rule, the cooler the weather the longer the time to maturity, so it might be a good idea to consult your seedman at the time of purchase to get the right seed for the time of year. Seeds are sown from mid-September through January. Seeds may be sown directly into the ground in rows 10 cm apart, thinning out later also to about 10 cm apart. I prefer, however, to sow the seeds in trays before transplanting them out to their final positions. This is mainly because of space conservation and time saving if the garden is still occupied by other plants. An added advantage is that the seedlings can be taken under cover in case of a rainstorm.

Feed every two weeks with a liquid fertiliser. Harvest with a sharp knife, leaving two or three side shoots for a second picking.

Choi sum

CHRYSANTHEMUM VEGETABLE

(Tong hao, Garland chrysanthemum, Edible chrysanthemum, Crown daisy) 茼蒿 | *Chrysanthemum coronarium*

Greater tong hao

Lesser tong hao

Lesser tong hao in flower

A native of the Mediterranean region, this vegetable is now grown for food throughout China. Two cultivars are commonly grown: the greater (large leaf) tong hao 茼蒿 and the lesser (narrow leaf) tong hao 皇帝菜, also known as Japanese tong hao 日本茼蒿. The former has deeply lobed, wrinkled leaves and short petioles. Although rather squat in appearance, it will reach about 15 cm at harvest time. Sow in trays from October through January, then transplant out when about 7 cm high, about 10 cm apart each way. The plants are picked whole, while still young, and should be ready in about five weeks. Left to grow to maturity it becomes a sprawling but tall leafy plant bearing simple, cream flowers with a yellow centre. The aromatic light green leaves have a distinctive herbal taste that may not appeal to all. It can be stir-fried but is most popular in hot-pots when it is briefly dipped in hot broth before eating.

The lesser tong hao is less familiar to most people but is increasing in popularity. It has thinner deeply dissected leaves, and has a more upright posture, 15–20 cm high at harvest time. This variety is much simpler to grow and has a longer growing season than most leafy green vegetables. The sowing can begin in early September and extend to mid-March. Sow the seeds broadcast, direct in the growing site. No transplanting is needed, simply thin out the seedlings as they begin to crowd (about two weeks from sowing) and use the thinnings at the table. This is a rapidly growing plant needing very little care and should be ready for the table in four to five weeks. The lesser tong hao is not picked whole: harvest by cutting what you need. A further three or four harvests will extend its useful production to six to ten weeks.

Similar in taste to its cousin, it is less pungent and can be eaten raw as a very useful, if little known salad vegetable. I have tested it many times on unsuspecting visitors, usually with favourable results. Because of its versatility, this is my preferred variety of tong hao.

CUCUMBER 青瓜 | *Cucumis sativus*

This versatile vegetable is a warm weather crop and should be started in March. A suitable support is necessary for this vine which climbs by means of tendrils. A suitable trellis should be erected, conveniently of bamboo, and forming any structural design that appeals to you—a wigwam or a row or a lean-to arrangement. A fence, if available is very suitable.

The seeds should be planted at the base of a support, 2 cm deep, four seeds at each site. Equally acceptable is to start the seeds in 7-cm plastic pots. As the seedlings appear, select the strongest to grow on. It should be ready for transplanting when about 10 cm tall. Allow two lateral shoots to appear, then stop the leader by pinching it off. Male and female flowers form on the same plant. I prefer to hand pollinate if possible, for more consistent results. To do this, pick a male flower and remove all its petals in order to expose the pollen-covered stamens. Take this along to an open female flower and apply the pollen onto the protruding stigma, thereby performing the task of pollination. Allow three or four fruits on each plant. Cucumber is a valued salad vegetable but is equally suitable for cooking. Thinly sliced it makes a very tasty pickle. The miniature variety, the gherkin, is the size of a fat finger and is especially suitable for pickling whole.

Cucumber

Gherkin

EGGPLANT (Aubergine, Brinjal) 矮瓜 / 茄子 | *Solanum melongena*

In her *Food Plants of China*, S.Y. Hu notes: "The introduction of the cultivated eggplant into China was through ethnobotanical channels. Ancient Chinese records show that it came both overland by the silk route and in an unrecorded manner of cultural diffusion among the Asian peoples. It was first recorded in AD 609 in the *Miscellaneous Records of Daye Reign* (AD 605–617) of Sui Dynasty as Gourd-of-the-Kunlun Mountain, a name which indicates the exact direction of its movement overland from West to East."

Eggplant

Long purple

Eggplant is a tropical vegetable native to Asia. It prefers warm conditions but can be successfully grown in Hong Kong winters although growth slows down considerably in January and February. It is usually grown as an annual, but healthy plants can sometimes be kept for two or three years. The plant is a sturdy, erect shrub about 60 cm high, with semi-woody stems that may be thorny. At the height of its growth, axillary shoots are produced, many of which should be pinched out to avoid a plant heavy with foliage but with few fruits. The leaves are ovate, irregularly lobed and the flowers a rich purple. The best-known eggplant is the familiar pendulous, slightly curved, shiny, deep purple

Round eggplant

Orange eggplant

fruit—a thing of such beauty as to be a feast for the eyes as well as for the palate. This remains my favourite eggplant even though other varieties abound, with colours from white to orange and shapes from flat to round.

White eggplant

Sow the seeds from April through July, four seeds to a 7-cm pot or paper cup. After the second leaf appears, thin out all but the strongest seedling. When the roots fill the pot, transplant into the ground 40 cm apart each way. A 25-cm pot will comfortably host a single plant. Pick the fruit young, while still springy to the touch, usually about 12 cm long. I often have trouble with mealy bugs which I physically remove by rubbing while wearing cotton gloves. Some light staking is often useful if the plant is laden with fruit and starts to show signs of toppling.

Eggplant has a low energy value of about 30 kcal per 100 g and is therefore useful in weight-reducing diets.

FIG 無花果 | *Ficus carica*

Ficus is a huge genus of some 800 species in tropical and subtropical regions of the world, of which the most familiar in Hong Kong is our beloved Chinese banyan tree. But of this large group only the *F. carica* is suitable for human consumption. It is indigenous to Turkey and Western Asia and enjoys a sunny climate with warm, dry summers.

Fig

With our very wet summers, Hong Kong may not be the ideal environment for figs but they nonetheless do fairly well if protected from the heavy summer rains. I recently visited an organic farm in the northern New Territories where a start-up fig orchard (under cover) seems to be doing very well, growing "Brown Turkey" (large purplish-brown fruit with pink flesh) and "Genoa" (greenish-yellow fruit with amber flesh). This is the first venture I know that produces fresh figs for the Hong Kong market and it has yet to make an impact outside of the hotels and boutique restaurants that it supplies. I hope the situation will change but until then, why don't we grow our own?

A small, deciduous tree up to 4 m high, it has distinctive large, ovate leaves, 3–5-lobed, rough to the touch. A large urn will do very well in a sunny position but some way should be found to protect it from heavy rains in the summer. Prune away any roots that escape the pot. Keep well mulched with compost and avoid cultivating the surface excessively as it is easy to damage the roots. It is said that the fig grows best if the roots are confined: this should make it suited to containers.

The flowers are confined within the cavity of the fig itself and are therefore not visible. This accounts for its Chinese name of "fruit without flowers". The so-called "fruit" is in fact a fleshy, hollow branch containing within it numerous tiny flowers and fruits on the inside. A small hole at the broad end of the fig—the ostiole—allows small wasps to enter and perform their pollinating function. In the late summer, fruits are produced singly in the leaf axils, and when ripe, will begin to droop and soften significantly—this is the time to pick it. Some protection from birds, such as netting, may be necessary. The shrub enters a rest phase in the winter, and even though some fruits are produced, they show little inclination to develop and ripen.

Figs and other summer fruit (papaya and wampi)

Propagation is easy in the spring or summer from heel cuttings. In the spring, prune any damaged branches and remove surplus shoots any time during the growing season. Figs may also be grown from seeds although this is a more laborious task.

A delicious syrup can be prepared from fig leaves. This makes a refreshing summer drink when iced or a soothing winter drink served hot. Very soothing for the throat. Please refer to the section on recipes.

GUAVA 蕃石榴 | *Psidium guajava*

Guava bark

Guava fruit

This small tropical evergreen tree, up to 5 m tall, is found all over Hong Kong especially in old gardens and in the wild. Its trunk has a very distinctive appearance, covered with blotchy areas that peel off in patches, each patch a different shade of brown or cream. The wood is extremely hard, and was once valued as tools for grinding or pounding. As young boys, my friends and I were always on the lookout for suitably shaped branches of guava wood for the making of catapults.

Its fruit is a round or oval berry, about 5 cm across, green turning to yellow with tinges of pink. Its delicious flesh surrounds hundreds of small, hard seeds packed in the centre which just happens to be the sweetest part of the whole fruit. When ripe it has an intense fragrance that can be detected from some distance.

The local guava is not grown commercially, but small quantities appear at local markets in the late summer. The commercial, shop-bought guava is sourced from Southeast Asia and Australia. Sometimes referred to as apple guava, it is nothing like the original, being much larger, harder in consistency and much less intense in taste. Strangely, it is also completely devoid of the all-important fragrance. Apart from being eaten fresh, guava is made into jam, juice and jelly. The guava is something of a super fruit in terms of nutrition, being very high in fibre and with four times the vitamin C content of an orange.

Propagation is from seed or air-layering.

A miniature herb garden

HERBS 香草

Used here, the term "herb" is regarded not in a botanical, but rather a culinary sense. Herbs are often grown by people who may grow nothing else, even in confined spaces such as a kitchen window sill or a verandah—easy access for the cook. For those with gardens, it is common for herbs to be grown in a dedicated area, a "herb garden", which if properly put together has great ornamental qualities. In my own garden I grow almost all my herbs in pots strung up on a fence—my "herb fence". Here I describe only those herbs which I have personally grown in Hong Kong with reasonable success.

Arugula (Rocket, Roquette) 芝麻菜 | *Eruca versicaria* syn. *E. sativa*

Arugula

This low-growing, compact annual is very popular as a salad green especially in Europe. It has a very strong, sharp and peppery taste, and should only be used in small quantities mixed with other salad vegetables. The young leaves are best, as the older ones become tough and overly pungent. It is not always available in Hong Kong and when available, is very expensive to buy. Yet it is very simple to grow and perfect as a pot plant. Start the plants in October. Sow the seeds, say about ten, into a 15-cm pot, and cover with a very thin layer of soil. Watch out for snails. I always leave one or two plants to grow on for seed collection which I use the following year. It never fails.

Basil (Sweet basil) 薰蕁/九層塔 | *Ocimum basilicum*

Sweet basil

Basil seems to be everyone's favourite "western" herb. However, its heritage is not European, being African, Asian and Middle Eastern in origin. It is steeped in religious history and is said to have grown around Jesus' tomb at the time of the resurrection.

Basil is now widely grown all over the world for its highly aromatic leaves used for sauces, salads, stews and curries. Fortunately, it is one of the easiest herbs to grow and can be grown throughout the year. Its leaves are opposite, mostly oval. Small tubular flowers are borne in whorls around the ends of the stems. Seeds are produced in abundance and can be saved for the following year. Basil is an annual, but occasionally a plant can be kept for a further year or more if it is noted to be robust. Seeds can be sown any time of the year and it is an ideal pot plant for the verandah or kitchen window sill. A single plant will grow well in a 15-cm pot. When the plant is 10 cm tall, pinch out the growing tip to allow lateral spread. Pinch out any flower buds unless you wish to save seeds.

There are many cultivars of basil selected for differences in colour, fragrance and flavour. A very popular variant is Thai basil which has narrower leaves and a stronger

Purple basil

Thai basil

flavour reminiscent of cloves. This is of course the basil of choice for Thai cooking. I have also grown purple-leaf basil and Greek basil. The latter is important in the Greek Orthodox tradition where it is used to perfume holy water. All types of basil are easy to grow and taste vastly better than the dried variety sold in shops. Much of the taste of basil is lost in the drying process, but an alternative method of keeping the leaves is to preserve them in olive oil. By far the best use for fresh basil is to make pesto. Please refer to the recipe section.

Bay leaves (Bay laurel, Sweet laurel) 月桂 | *Laurus nobilis*

Traditionally in western civilisation, a crown was fashioned of interwoven laurel branches and awarded to athletes or poets as a mark of achievement. Is it still done, I wonder?

Bay leaves

In Hong Kong bay leaves are mostly grown in pots, but if grown in the ground it can grow to a substantial shrub 2 m tall. Large pot-grown plants are also grown for ornamental purposes, sometimes as a standard and often clipped to fancy shapes. The dark green, shiny leaves have a leathery texture and when crushed, give off a wonderful fragrance not found in the dried, shop-bought leaves. Culinary uses are mainly for soups and stews. Scale is a frequent problem, which I wipe out with a gloved hand or a toothbrush. I once had a bad infestation of whiteflies. My sister, an accomplished gardener living abroad, suggested I plant a few cloves of garlic around it. Presto: no more whiteflies.

Propagation may be from seeds, but these are difficult to obtain. The plants can also be raised from semi-ripe cuttings, but the strike rate is not high and growth is slow. It would be best to buy a small plant from a nursery if one is available.

Chinese chives (Garlic chives) 韭菜 | *Allium tuberosum*

Cultivated for centuries in India and China, this useful clump-forming herb is easily started from seed. Once established, it will last forever, providing you with chives winter and summer, and will tolerate frequent cutting. Sow the seeds in the ground or in a pot from April through to September. Its leaves are dark green, long and flat. The leaves, chopped up, are a common ingredient in dumplings. It can be used as a substitute for spring onions and is useful as a green vegetable, usually combined with others. The flowering spike is also a valuable and popular vegetable.

Blanched Chinese chives 韭黃 is a sought-after vegetable, produced by placing special pots or "chimneys" to cut out light. Actually any suitable dark-coloured receptacle will work just as well. The result is a more tender, light yellow-green product that tastes quite different from the green version. Once established, chives are readily propagated by division of the clumps.

Green and blanched chives

Method of blanching

Coriander (Cilantro) 芫荽 | *Coriandrum sativum*

Coriander

Often mistaken for parsley, it is sometimes referred to as "Chinese parsley". It is my favourite "local" herb though I know some people who cannot stand it. The leaves, raw or lightly cooked, are used in a host of different dishes, but especially in steamed food. The roots are also used for flavouring and the seeds are ground up to a powder and used in curries, chutneys and even cakes. Sow the seeds from late September through January. The seeds are large and may take a while to germinate. This can be overcome by soaking the seed overnight before sowing. In the markets the plant is sold whole, but the home gardener can economise by picking the leaves as and when required, thus extending the production life of the plant. Several sowings are necessary to cover the whole winter season.

Curry leaves 調料九里香/茄苳葉 | *Murraya koenigii*

Curry leaves

The English word "curry" comes from the Tamil "kari" which means a "sauce". The leaves of this species are used in South Asian curries and other dishes. They are not easily bought, except in specialist shops, and then only the dried version is available. The plant is related to mock orange (orange jessamine) (*M. paniculata*), widespread in Hong Kong as a garden ornamental.

The curry leaf plant is a shrub or small tree with compound leaves comprising 17–31 toothed leaflets. When crushed the leaves give out an intense aroma. Loose sprays of fragrant, creamy white flowers produce green berries which will eventually turn black when ripe. Propagation is not difficult from seed. Cuttings are also possible but not reliable. Offshoots around the base of the shrub may also be carefully dug up and potted on.

Dill 蒔蘿 | *Anethum graveolens*

Dill

Dill flowers

Dill is a herb occurring wild in Europe and temperate Asia. Long hollow stalks, up to 60 cm or more, carry wispy, fern-like foliage very similar to fennel. Umbels of aromatic yellow flowers are followed by pungent seeds. Better though, for the home gardener to use the foliage before the flowers appear. The dried foliage is usually referred to as 'dill weed' and has a milder flavour. Dill is used in myriad ways, especially in pickles and fish dishes. The well-known Nordic delicacy, gravlax (or gravadlax) is made from raw salmon cured with salt, sugar and lots of dill. My favourite way to use it is to sprinkle the fresh herb onto poached salmon. Note that its flavour is rapidly destroyed by heat, so it should not be subjected to the high temperatures of cooking.

You may wish to use dill as a cure for hiccups as did the ancient Greeks. They also used it as a love potion—you may wish to try that out too. Otherwise, go easy on the gravlax.

Sow the seeds in October for best results.

Fennel 茴香 | *Foeniculum vulgare*

This aromatic herb is grown for its very finely cut, aniseed-flavoured leaves, much favoured for fish dishes. *F. vulgare* var. *azoricum* or Florence fennel is grown for its swollen stems, with the consistency of celery, for use as a vegetable. Its leaves can also be used in the same way as common fennel. Grown from seed as a cool season crop, it has a rapid growth habit and is ready for the table in about eight weeks.

Florence fennel

Galangal (Sand ginger) 高良薑/沙薑 | *Kaempferia galanga*

Galangal

This is a lesser-known ginger but important nevertheless in Chinese, Thai and Indian cooking. The plant is valued for its root, which is usually sold in the dried, powdered form. In Chinese cooking it is most commonly used to flavour steamed chicken. Galangal can be grown in a pot from pieces of the fresh rhizome. The leaves first appear tightly furled then open up to an almost round shape. It makes good progress in the summer then almost dies down in the winter. The dry powder is a component of many traditional Chinese medicinal potions and has been used in Africa to treat malaria.

Garlic 蒜 | *Allium sativum*

Garlic

This hardy perennial herb of the onion family is grown for its strong flavour. It could be the most used herb of all time. In California alone, the harvest amounts to several hundred million kilos annually. Above the ground, it resembles onion closely but below, the bulb is compound and is made up of several cloves encased by layers of papery sheaths. Start garlic by planting individual cloves in October, flat end down with the nose just below the soil. Pinch off the flower heads as they appear so as to divert all the nutrients to the bulbs. The growing period is very long, five months or so, and is ready for harvest when the leaves wilt. Interplanting with garlic has some value in discouraging aphids and whiteflies.

Garlic has a huge market as a therapeutic agent. It is a repository of a great number of active chemical substances. Herbalists have for centuries utilised garlic for a wide variety of ailments and the list is growing still. Long before the discovery of antibiotics, garlic was known to have antibacterial properties and has been used for this purpose both internally and externally. Numerous research papers report on the effectiveness of garlic in improving circulation. It acts as an antioxidant to protect blood vessels from free radicals, lowers low-density lipoproteins, cleans out blood vessels by the process of fibrinolysis, and reduces the risk of cancers. This is as close as you can get to a panacea, if you are to believe it all.

Ginger 薑 | *Zingiber officinale*

Ginger is a pungent tropical perennial herb, an absolute essential in Chinese cooking. It is spicy to the taste but soothing to the digestive tract. Ginger is grown for its irregular, creeping underground rhizome which is used to flavour all manner of dishes. Its leaves are narrow, lanceolate but its flowers are seldom seen. The young rhizome has a crispy texture and is harvested in mid-growth for use as a vegetable and for preserves. The older root is hard and fibrous and is used sliced, julienned or crushed to flavour food. Ginger needs a light soil for the rhizomes to develop properly. Propagation is by division of the rhizome in the early spring.

Ginger

Ginger has been and continues to be widely used as a therapeutic agent. In the tradition of Ayurvedic medicine, it was known as the "great or universal medicine". It was so valued in the Middle Ages that it was thought to originate from the Garden of Eden. The Romans ate ginger to cure or prevent intestinal parasites.

In modern medicine, there is good evidence that ginger relieves digestive complaints such as nausea, motion sickness, morning sickness, and the nausea and vomiting of chemotherapy. This could be due to the chemicals gingerols and shagoals found in ginger, which stimulate the outflow of saliva, bile and gastric secretions. In addition, it promotes gentle muscle contractions that help normal transit through the digestive tract. Preliminary studies also suggest that ginger lowers cholesterol, and acts as an antioxidant to prevent arterial plaque and platelet aggregation that can lead to thrombosis.

Lemon balm 香蜂草 | *Melissa officinalis*

Lemon balm

This herb, in the mint family, is grown for its fresh lemon-scented and lemon-flavoured leaves. The light yellow-green leaves are deeply crinkled and a light touch with the fingers is all that is needed to release its strong scent. As a culinary herb it is used to flavour ices, jellies, tea and summer drinks. It can be used as a substitute for lemon peel. Rubbing the leaves on the skin is said to prevent insect bites. Lemon balm grows readily in the summer but may die down completely in the winter only to spring up again with the return of warm weather. Sow seeds in the spring.

Lemongrass 香茅 | *Cymbopogon citratus*

Lemongrass

Lemongrass is native to India and now grows well in any warm, tropical climate. It forms a dense clump of long, grey-green leaves that resemble many rank roadside grasses. I have never seen it flower. It is grown for its fleshy white bases used in Southeast Asian cooking, especially Thai cuisine. When crushed, the whole plant gives off a strong fragrance of lemon and it is for this that it is valued in cooking. I suggest growing them in large 30-cm pots to prevent an unruly invasion. They soon crowd out their pots and when they do, divide the plants for propagation. I have never had any problems with pests or disease. It is very easy to grow, and is available for harvest throughout the year.

Lemongrass has been used in traditional medicine in Indonesia, Malaysia and India for centuries. Ayurvedic practitioners chiefly used lemongrass in the form of a tea infusion for combating fevers, and nervous and digestive disorders. It has also been used externally for the relief of rheumatic pains, ringworm, scabies and lice. It is believed to have mild tranquilising properties.

Several closely related members of the *Cymbopogon* genus are cultivated for their oils, some of which are used in the perfume industry. Citronella oil, widely used as an insect repellent, especially against mosquitoes, is prepared from *C. nardus*.

Lemon-scented geranium 怕蚊草/檸檬天竺葵 | *Pelargonium crispum*

Lemon-scented geranium

Lemon-scented geranium (so-called, although it does not belong to the *Geranium* genus) is one of several varieties of scented geraniums. This perennial has a bushy habit and is grown mainly for its decorative, thick, hairy leaves which are deeply dissected. Scattered pink or mauve flowers are an added attraction. Scented geraniums have glands at the base of their leaf hairs where the scent is formed. Bruising or crushing the leaves releases a strong and distinctive lemony scent. Propagation is by soft cuttings in the spring or early summer. Avoid over-watering which may lead to rot.

This is an edible plant, although its leaves are too rough to be palatable. It is better used to flavour ices and jellies. When expecting guests, I often insert the bruised leaves into folded napkins. The release of its scent is an unexpected and pleasant surprise when the napkins are unfolded for use. The flowers are edible and may be used to garnish salads.

The Chinese appellation 怕蚊草 implies that this plant deters mosquitoes. It does not, despite the assurances of shopkeepers at the Mongkok flower market. The name might be more appropriately applied to *P. citrosum* which, though having a strong citronella scent, also has no effect on mosquitoes. However, citronella oil, which does have some deterrent properties against mosquitoes, is sourced from an entirely unrelated plant, *Cymbopogon nardus* (see under 'Lemongrass'), and is extensively exploited commercially for this purpose. The home gardener, anxious to deter mosquitoes, would be much better served by planting the humble marigold because of its Pyrethrum content, which is an ingredient in countless insect repellant preparations.

Mint 薄荷 | *Mentha*

This aromatic perennial, evergreen herb, of which there are 25 species, spreads widely through creeping overground and underground stolons. This habit makes it potentially invasive but also makes it useful as ground cover. The most commonly grown species in Hong Kong is spearmint (*M. spicata*) although field mint (*M. arvensis*) and peppermint (*M. piperita*) are grown all over China. All species share an intense aroma of the crushed leaves although there are subtle differences. The leaves are elliptical, opposite, serrated and may be slightly downy. Its complex venation gives it a somewhat quilted look. Propagate by cuttings or by division. The plants grow to about 20 cm (apple mint or *M. sauveolens* grows to 70 cm or more) and survive repeated pruning throughout the year. Pot plants do very well.

Mint

Mint is cultivated mostly for its flavour and fragrance but it also has uses in medicine and in industry. As a flavouring, its uses are well-known. Mint tea is a delicious and popular drink: lightly crush a handful of fresh mint leaves and place them in a teapot. Pour in boiling hot tea, separately prepared, using any type of tea that you fancy. Add some sugar for taste and serve after five minutes. Mint sauce for lamb dishes is much superior when made with fresh mint leaves. Mint julep, a popular cocktail in the southern United States is made from mint leaves, crushed ice, sugar and bourbon.

Medicinal uses abound. Menthol is prepared from mint oils and has value in promoting digestion, as a counter-irritant and as a decongestant, for example in the common cold. Peppermint oil is a recognised and effective treatment for symptoms of the irritable bowel syndrome. It works by relieving intestinal spasm and flatulence and is now extensively used in modern medicine. The cosmetic industry uses mint in perfumes, shampoos, lip balms and aromatherapy.

Oregano (Sweet marjoram) 牛至 | *Origanum majorana*

Oregano

Oregano flowers

This is another herb difficult to obtain fresh. It hails from the Mediterranean regions and grows as a compact, rounded perennial shrub about 20 cm high, bearing small, mid-green heart-shaped leaves. Bunches of pale pink flowers cluster at the end of the branches. Grown in a pot, it has a semi-trailing habit and is quite decorative and particularly suited to rock gardens. The highly aromatic leaves have a special affinity with tomatoes and go well with many meats, especially lamb. Best started from seed sown in October. The plant will last for years.

Pandan leaves 香蘭葉 | *Pandanus amaryllifolius*

Pandan leaves

Pandanus belongs to the family of screw pines many of which grow wild along Hong Kong's seashores. Some bear fruits that are an aggregation of berries resembling pineapples and are edible. However, this is the only species with fragrant leaves. This palm-like evergreen is native to tropical Asia and pandan leaves have an important role as a flavouring agent in Southeast Asian cooking—especially in Malaysia, Thailand, Indonesia and the Philippines. However, it has no significant place in Chinese cooking.

It has long sprays of narrow, shiny blade-like leaves which, unlike other varieties of pandanus, do not have spiny edges. Woody aerial roots are prominent. The plants are sterile and need to be raised from cuttings. The leaves have a nutty, botanical fragrance and are used to flavour rice and cakes. In Thai cooking, pieces of chicken are wrapped in the leaves for frying. The leaves may also be used in weaving.

On a personal note, although I do have a pandan leaf plant in my garden given to me by a Singaporean neighbour, I must admit that I seldom use it, as I find it does not live up to its billing. It may be possible that locally grown plants do not have the same aromatic qualities as those grown in a truly tropical environment.

Parsley 洋芫荽 | *Petroselinum crispum*

Parsley is one of the most essential and loved herbs in western cuisine. It also makes a decorative foliage plant and is ideal for pot culture and for garnish. The most commonly used forms are the curly-leafed form, densely curled and moss-like, or the stronger, flat-leafed Italian parsley (*P. crispum* var. *Neapolitanum*) with flat, triangular leaves each divided into many leaflets with toothed margins. The latter is my preferred variety which I grow every year in the cool season. It is a biennial, but is best used as an annual. Sow the seeds directly into a 25-cm pot—about 20 seeds. Leave three plants to grow to maturity into clumps. One sowing will provide a steady supply of parsley for the whole season.

Italian parsley

Curly-leafed parsley

Rosemary 迷迭香 | *Rosmarinus officinalis*

Rosemary

Rosemary is a small evergreen shrub native to the Mediterranean. It has narrow needle-like leaves that are dark green and extremely aromatic. Simply stroking the plant will release its powerful fragrance. In Hong Kong it may grow to about 1 m. Being quite attractive it can even be used as a hedge as it tolerates regular clipping well. Rosemary does well in poor soil but will not survive overwatering. Torrential summer rains have taken a heavy toll on my shrubs in the past, so it is important to provide a light soil with good drainage. A good idea is to grow them in pots which can be spirited away under cover in case of storms. Another good idea is to keep raising new plants from cuttings so as to have ready replacements just in case. Rosemary is one of my personal favourite herbs which I find goes particularly well with potatoes, lamb or chicken.

Traditionally, rosemary has been linked to preserving memory. Ancient Greek scholars would wear garlands of rosemary around their necks during examinations to improve memory and concentration. Ophelia said, "*There's rosemary, that's for remembrance,*" (*Hamlet,* IV: 5). This property of rosemary may not be entirely fanciful as modern research is investigating whether its antioxidant and anti-inflammatory actions may be useful in slowing the progress of Alzheimer's disease.

Sesame flowers

Sesame pods and seeds

Sage 鼠尾草 | *Salvia officinalis*

As the name suggests, sage is a form of Salvia. It takes the form of a shrubby perennial. Its four-sided stem bears stalked, ovate, grey-green leaves that have a wrinkled appearance. It is readily raised from seed or cuttings and does well in poor soil. It is well suited to pot culture. (See photo paired with Thyme.)

Sesame 芝麻 | *Sesamum orientale*

I was once given some seeds of black sesame which I grew out of curiosity. It is unlikely that the home gardener can grow enough of it to be of practical use. Sesame is grown for its seeds, which are used to flavour bread, cakes and savouries. The oil is of great value in cooking all over Asia and no Hong Kong kitchen should be without it. Ground sesame seeds are used to prepare the creamy "tahini" so important in Middle Eastern cooking. Hummus is a mixture of tahini and chickpeas.

The sesame plant is an annual growing to about 50 cm. It has mid-green lanceolate leaves and axillary white flowers. At a glance it could be mistaken for the balsam plant. The flowers develop into pods each containing a large number of seeds, black or white according to the variety. The pods, green at first, harden and dry to a dark brown. They must be harvested before they split and scatter the seeds. Have you ever wondered about the origin of the command "Open sesame!" from the *Arabian Nights*? Now you have your answer!

Spring onion 蔥 | *Allium cepa*

Spring onion in flower

Purple spring onion

This is arguably the most commonly used local herb. Found in every wet market, a few sprigs are customarily handed out as a parting gift for every vegetable purchase. It is impossible to imagine Chinese cuisine without it. Seeds can be sown in the cool weather, but it is so much easier to start from bulbs (shallots). To keep up a small home supply, it would be even easier if the lower bulbous portion of the mature plant is re-planted into small pots. Progress from day one is amazing—a centimetre every day. Cut the tops off for use as required, and it will keep coming. It is highly recommended for first-time herb growers with nothing more than a window sill.

Thyme 百里香 | *Thymus*

Thyme (left) and sage

The ancient Egyptians used thyme for embalming. Greeks used it for scenting baths and as a burnt incense in temples. Traditionally thyme has associations with strength, courage and well-being. As a culinary herb it is valued for its strong flavour and for its easy blending with other spices. It is an important ingredient in bouquet garni and herbes de Provence. The herb is mostly bought in the dried form and I have only rarely seen it sold fresh. The plant is a low-growing perennial composed of woody sprigs to which are attached paired tiny leaves or flowers. It is easily raised from seed in the cool season or from cuttings. It is an ideal pot-grown herb that is also suited to rock gardens.

Its strong flavour is due to the presence of the chemical thymol. Thymol has antiseptic properties and is the main ingredient in Listerine mouthwash.

Turmeric 黄薑 | *Curcuma domestica* syn. *C. longa*

Turmeric

This perennial rhizomatous herb belongs to the ginger family Zingiberaceae and is believed to have originated in tropical South Asia. Turmeric is grown for its mildly spicy rhizomes, very similar in appearance to ginger. It is mostly sold as a bright orange powder which is an essential ingredient in curry powder, chutneys and pickles. It is also widely used as a very satisfactory substitute for the very expensive saffron and as a colouring for mustard preparations. Fresh turmeric is hard to come by, but can sometimes be found in farmers' markets. The fresh version, thinly sliced or crushed, can be used in any recipe that calls for the powdered variety. There is very little difference in terms of taste, but a subtle fragrance is the advantage of the fresh root. Turmeric is grown from a piece of rhizome in the spring or early summer, and should be harvested when the leaves die down in about nine months' time.

Turmeric has been used in traditional Ayurvedic medicine for multiple ailments. It is said to have antibacterial powers and as such, is used to dress cuts and wounds. Modern medicine is actively investigating the use of curcumin, the molecule believed to be responsible for its actions. Trials are under way to determine its use in minimising the death of brain cells following a stroke.

Curcumin could also be the explanation for the so-called "Indian enigma". The occurrence of stomach cancer is highest in those countries that have a high incidence of infection of the stomach by an organism known as *Helicobacter pylori*. In India the rate of infection is high but the incidence of stomach cancer is paradoxically low. One theory is that the high consumption of turmeric in Indian curries and other foods has a protective effect.

KAI CHOI (Leaf mustard, Mustard greens, Swatow mustard)

芥菜 / 大芥菜 | *Brassica juncea*

This is one of the less popular Chinese leafy greens, but it is valuable because it can be grown throughout the year. Summer crops are less luxuriant and are more susceptible to infestation by aphids. I usually grow this towards the end of the cool season, around March, when the other leafy greens such as choi sum are winding down.

The vegetable is a uniform green throughout, with loose erect leaves not forming a heart. It is harvested before the appearance of the flowering spike. It is sold whole in markets but again the home gardener may harvest the individual leaves to extend the production life of the plant.

Kai choi

I sow the seeds in trays and transplant out when 7 cm high in rows 20 cm apart. You may also sow broadcast and thin as required.

I must now add kai choi to my list of salad greens. I had always eaten it stir-fried with ginger and never raw, believing the sharp taste to be a little overpowering. However I have recently been told by a gardener friend who had just returned from a trip to Central America, that raw mustard greens are a common and delicious addition to salads in that part of the world. I put away my old prejudices and tried it again: it's true—it does add a certain dimension, much in the way that the sharp shock of arugula livens up a salad.

Swatow kai choi

Swatow mustard 大芥菜 (*B. juncea* var. *rugosa*) is a variety of kai choi with the difference that it does form a heart. This is a much larger plant and is sold with the outer leaves removed. It has a slight bitter taste which I find appealing, and is best stir-fried with a sliver of ginger. Swatow mustard makes an excellent pickle—check out the recipe section.

KAI LAN (Chinese flowering kale) 芥蘭 | *Brassica alboglabra*

Together with choi sum and pak choi, kai lan completes the top three of the long list of Chinese leafy vegetables. It is thought to be indigenous to South China but its growth form and white flowers make it a close relative of the Portuguese cabbages. The oval leaves are greenish-blue, thick and waxy with a fine whitish bloom. The succulent central stalk bears racemes of white flowers and is harvested just as the flowers begin to open. A smaller second harvest may be obtained from side shoots.

Kai lan

Kai lan is a cool season crop and seeds can be sown from mid-September through January. Start in trays and plant out when about 7 cm tall 10 cm apart each way. It can also be sown directly where it is to grow in rows 15 cm apart and thinned out as required.

Kai lan should always be lightly cooked with ginger, a little sugar and a splash of Chinese rice wine. The succulent stalks can be peeled and cut in rings for use as a substitute for the more expensive asparagus.

KOHL RABI 芥蘭頭 | *Brassica oleracea* var. *caulorapa*

Kohl rabi

Kohl rabi is closely related to kai lan and is grown for its crisp, globular, swollen stems that are just above ground level. The name is derived from the German "kohl" (cabbage) and "rübi" (turnip). Often mistaken for a turnip, it is light green in colour but a purple variety is also grown. A winter vegetable, it can be sown from October through January. I usually grow kohl rabi late in the season when the winter leafy vegetables are coming to an end. It is best to start the seeds in sectioned trays or small pots, four seeds to a pot, leaving the strongest seedling to grow on and thinning the rest. Transplant to the ground when about 7 cm high. A single plant grows very well in a 23-cm pot. Harvest the globes when still young, not larger than a tennis ball. Older specimens become extremely fibrous. It is delicious sliced and stir-fried with garlic but it can also be cut into strips and eaten raw in salads.

LEEK 大蒜 | *Allium porrum*

Leek

This is a member of the onion family, but it does not form a bulb. Instead, it has broad concave leaves that form a tight white cylinder at the base, this being the part that is eaten. The green leaves need not be wasted as they are useful in a vegetable soup. It is grown as a cool season crop, although I remember seeing it harvested on Lamma Island in mid-June. Sow the seeds in October into small plastic pots or cups and transplant out when about 7 cm high. Leek is a biennial and the growing season is quite long. In temperate climates it is often harvested well into the second year. However, it is more useful treated as an annual and it should be possible to achieve table size (when the stems grow to around 2.5 cm in diameter) in about five to six months.

In the year 640, the Welsh scored a famous victory over the Saxons. In that battle, the Welsh soldiers wore leeks in their helmets to distinguish themselves from their enemies. Ever since then, the leek has become one of the national emblems of Wales—the others being the daffodil and the red dragon.

LEMON 檸檬 | *Citrus limon*

The origin of this well-known and important fruit is shrouded in mystery, but is believed to be native to Northern India. It is a small tree, up to 4 m, much branched and protected by stiff, sharp thorns. The dark green leaves are alternate, simple, oval, and delightfully aromatic when crushed. Flowers appear in the spring. The unopened flowers are a light purple on the outside, cream-coloured when fully open, and mildly fragrant. The oval, yellow, very sour fruit hardly needs description, but a milder version, the "Meyer" lemon (possibly a cross between lemon and orange) is noticeably less acidic, a smaller size, less thorny, and better for containers. Fruits should be ready for picking in the late summer.

The original trees, so-called "rough" lemons (*C. jhambiri*), are no longer an important source of lemons having been superseded by newer cultivars. Nevertheless, they have a very useful role in providing robust and fast-growing rootstock for other citrus crops and plants to be grafted onto, such as the popular Chinese New Year tangerines. The fruit is twice the size of an ordinary lemon and entirely green with a thick knobbly skin. Sour like all lemons, it has in addition, a bitter hint. This combination makes for an exceptionally delicious lemonade even though it is less juicy than common lemons.

Lemon leaves are useful in cooking. The finely shredded leaves are an essential accompaniment to snake soup, a popular winter delicacy.

How I acquired a rough lemon tree is interesting. Some years ago I spotted this tree with green lemons in a garden in Kowloon. I started a conversation with the gardener within, who was lamenting his inability to afford fertiliser. A deal was struck: one bag of organic fertiliser in exchange for an air-layered lemon tree. This gentlemen's agreement had a happy conclusion a few months later and the tree is now contentedly growing in a planter in my garden and producing good fruit every year. In fact, rough lemons can be raised from seeds, and some, like the "Meyer", can be started from cuttings.

Lemon

Rough lemon: note the thick rind

Loose leaf lettuce

"Little Gem"

LETTUCE 生菜 | *Lactuca*

This could be perhaps the most satisfying of vegetables for the home gardener. It is indisputably the most important of the salad vegetables, all the more important if it is available for fresh picking. Lettuce is beloved of weight-watchers because of its low calorific value of a mere 18 kcal per 100 g.

Lactuca is a genus of about 100 species, best known in the form of the common lettuce. An ancient vegetable, it probably arose from the "prickly lettuce", a weed. There are many wild forms, some inedible and fiercely bitter. The most commonly eaten lettuce is *Lactuca sativa* and comes in a large number of shapes, sizes and flavours.

There are, loosely, four forms of lettuce. First, the heading or cabbage variety that produces a well-formed tight heart. Second, the upright cos or Romaine type which is oblong with crisper leaves and a sweeter flavour. Third, there is the loose-leaf variety with an open growth habit and the advantage that it is suited to the picking of the outer leaves as required. Fourth, the butterheads, a small variety with waxy light green outer leaves and a cream-coloured centre that may form into a distinct heart.

Leaf and cos lettuce are the easiest to grow. Butterheads do quite well but I have had less success with the heading types such as "Iceberg" which need cooler weather than we have here. The gardener has such a huge number of choices that all I can do is to encourage you to try something different every year. Easiest to grow is what is known in seed shops as "local" leaf lettuce but which is sourced from from all around the world. Romaine is a good choice as well, especially the miniature "Little Gem", which is one type I grow every year. This small lettuce can be grown to maturity in a small 12-cm pot and can be placed on window sills or hung up on fences. The leaves are crunchy and the firm heart especially delicious. Fancy leaf forms or red leaf varieties such as "Lollo Rossa" and "Quattro Stagioni" are well worth a trial. A locally popular lettuce, yau muk choi 油墨菜 has long, crunchy sword-shaped leaves useful in salads but is mostly eaten cooked.

Yau muk choi

Lettuce is a cool season crop started in late September for sowing through January. It does poorly in hot weather and while it can survive in the summer if protected from the worst heat, it is of poor quality. The seeds are preferably sown in open or sectioned trays like the other green vegetables described above. The seedlings can then be transplanted when 5 cm high to their growing positions. If grown in pots, it is best to grow singly in pots of a size suited to the chosen variety but it is never necessary to use

Red leaf lettuce

Quattro Stagioni

a pot of a larger diameter than 20 cm. Good drainage is essential, but pot plants dry out quite easily and care must be taken to keep them adequately watered. A liquid fertiliser or a sprinkling of organic fertiliser pellets should be applied every two weeks. Aphids can be a problem, and should be treated with a water spray with or without soap. Aphids can also be manually wiped off.

One species of lettuce close to my heart is a local (or Southern Chinese) variety known as fu muk choi 苦墨菜 or "bitter vegetable". It is very occasionally seen in wet markets but is generally not well-known except in rural villages. Its leaves are lanceolate but may be wide, narrow or dissected. The plants are quite large and may grow to 1 m. Traditionally it is prepared in the usual stir-fry manner, but I much prefer it raw as a salad vegetable, especially the type with the more fancy leaves. These leaves are crunchy, in particular the ribs. One great asset of fu muk choi is that it is one of the few lettuce varieties that can tolerate our hot summers. Hence, as summer approaches, and all our usual salad lettuces come to a seasonal end, fu muk choi steps in to fill the breach. Sow the seeds at winter's end or in the early spring. A second sowing about two months later should keep you in good supply for the whole season.

Romaine lettuce

For years I believed this plant to belong to the *Cichorium* genus since it has much in common with it: a slight bitter taste and a white sticky sap when injured. Moreover, my friends the Italian sisters used to love it and always referred to it as "cicoria". Determined to find out for sure, I sought advice from many sources but was given different information by different experts. Eventually, I was fortunate enough to arrange a visit with the world famous Professor S.Y. Hu at The Chinese University of Hong Kong. Professor Hu, who was then in her centennial year had just published a book *Food Plants of China*. Strangely there was no mention of this vegetable in her book. Laden with several pots of my precious vegetables I went off to see Professor Hu who took about two seconds to identify it as *Lactuca chinensis*. Thus ended my years-long quest.

Lactuca chinensis: 3 leaf forms

MANGO 芒果 | *Mangifera indica*

Mango in flower

The mango is native to the Indian sub-continent. It is a large evergreen tree that does best in the tropics but which is also cultivated successfully in sub-tropical parts of the world. In Hong Kong the tree is quite a common sight, found in old gardens, cemeteries and in the wild. Some survive as roadside trees even in the middle of the city.

In the markets in Hong Kong, two main varieties are seen, the Indian and the Philippine mango. The familiar rich-yellow Philippine fruit is the most plentiful and is superior in quality to the other imports from Australia, South Africa or Israel. Very few come from India itself, which is a shame since its "Alphonso" mango is one of the finest. What grows best locally is the Indian type. It is relatively easy to purchase a small container-grown tree already resplendent with fruit and this will live happily in a large container for years. Even without the fruit, the tree has value as an ornamental. The large, simple, elliptical dark green leaves may be 30 cm long.

Mangoes

Large clusters of very small, mildly fragrant flowers appear in the spring. The oval green fruit can be harvested in November, but ripening is sometimes erratic and with some trees they may not mature at all.

MATRIMONY VINE (Chinese boxthorn, Wolfberry, Goji berry)

枸杞 | *Lycium chinense*

This is a perennial shrub growing to about 1 m. It bears long, thorny, woody branches with dark green, alternate, ovate leaves. It is most luxuriant in the winter months but loses some of its leaves in the hot summer. In Southern China its berries do not develop while in the colder regions of Northern China, ellipsoid, 1.5 cm long, orange-red berries are harvested as a traditional medicinal herb. In my own garden I have seen blue flowers appear in small numbers, but no berries. In Hong Kong the leaves are stripped from the branches (being mindful of the thorns) and used as an ingredient for a light and very refreshing soup.

Matrimony vine

The vine thrives in ordinary soil and indeed is sometimes found growing wild in ditches. In late summer prune the branches to 10 cm from ground level, using the prunings as cuttings for propagation.

In recent years, the wolfberry or goji berry 杞子 has become a star attraction in alternative medicine, especially in the West. It is regarded as a near-panacea if all its claims are to be believed. Touted as a life-extending enhancer, and a general tonic, it is enjoying brisk sales in Europe and North America. In China, the berries and the roots have been used for centuries as a blood tonic, circulatory booster, a cure for tinnitus and dizziness, among others. In Chinese cooking it is mostly used as an ingredient in herbal soups. I have never seen the berries sold in the fresh state but the dried version is in plentiful supply in Chinese groceries or herbal shops.

The name "matrimony vine" has intrigued me, but I am still searching for its origin.

OKRA (Ladies' fingers, Gumbo) 羊角豆 / 毛茄 / 秋葵

Abelmoschus esculentus syn. *Hibiscus esculentus*

Okra "Clemson spineless"

Okra "Burgundy"

Okra, seed saving

This genus consists of about 15 species from tropical Asia and Africa. It used to be included in the larger *Hibiscus* genus. The plant is a fast-growing summer annual and may grow to 2 m, its stem reaching a diameter of 7–8 cm at the base. The large leaves are dissected into 3–7 lobes. A curious passer-by once questioned if I was growing cannabis—the leaves do have a vague resemblance since cannabis is also of the Hibiscus family! Beautiful pale yellow hibiscus-like flowers with a reddish-purple centre arise from each leaf axil, each one of which develops into an erect, light green pod resembling a large chilli. Reliable varieties are "Clemson spineless" and "Long green". I have also succeeded with "Burgundy" which produces a dark red pod that turns green when cooked.

A mature plant is very stately and attractive and would not be out of place as a backdrop in an ornamental garden. The growth rate of the pods, once they appear, is phenomenal—a pod not yet ready for picking in the morning may be ready in the afternoon. Pick the pods young, 7–8 cm long. Beyond this size, they rapidly become fibrous and cannot be eaten. The young pods contain numerous soft immature seeds in a mucilaginous matrix. This mucilage is useful in thickening soups and stews especially in the southern United States where okra is known as gumbo. The pods are covered with fine but sharp hairs and need to be handled with care.

Seeds can be collected from a mature pod for use the next season. The large mature seeds, when roasted and ground down, have been used as a coffee substitute. Okra is sometimes, but not regularly, found in wet markets but it is usually available in shops selling Indian or Thai provisions. Many locals are unfamiliar with okra but it is my favourite summer crop and I grow it every year. There are many ways to enjoy okra but I relish the pods most in curries or stews.

I start my plants in April or May by planting four seeds in a 12-cm pot. Always resist the temptation to start okra early, before it is warm enough—as I have learnt from failures over the years. Wait until the night-time temperature does not fall below 20°C. Germination takes place in a matter of four or five days. As the seedlings grow, thin out all but the strongest and plant out into the ground or a large pot, at least 30 cm in diameter. Grown in this way, the seedlings can always be protected from heavy seasonal rains that start about this time. The seeds can of course be sown where the plant is to grow, but this bears some risks of rain damage. Some staking for tall plants may be needed, though not always. A second sowing in July will ensure a supply to the end of October.

PAK CHOI (Chinese white cabbage) 白菜 | *Brassica chinensis*

Shanghai pak choi

Pak choi is one of the top triumvirate of Chinese vegetables, the other two being choi sum and kai lan. It is an Asian native widely cultivated in China. It is probably the most well-known Chinese vegetable in the West where it is sometimes referred to as bok choy.

There are two common cultivars: the "little" pak choi 小白菜, paradoxically, is the taller version growing to about 20 cm, while the "big" pak choi 大白菜 is squat with broader leaves and more succulent pure white petioles shaped like a Chinese spoon. Pak choi is most commonly sold before the central flowering spikes develop. However, if left to develop, the flowering spikes are sold as pak choi "flowers" 白菜花—this is probably the best tasting part of the vegetable. A special dwarf variety, "Hok Dao" pak choi 鶴藪白菜, is very much a local product, originating in a village of that name in the northern New Territories. This is a squat, quick-growing plant, about 6-8 cm

Little pak choi

Hok Dao pak choi

3 stages of drying pak choi

tall, ready for the table in four to six weeks. Another cultivar, the so-called Shanghai pak choi 上海白菜 has thinner, light green petioles. When served in restaurants, Shanghai pak choi often has its leaves trimmed away leaving only the clustered petioles for eating.

The taller type pak choi can also be dried for later use as a soup base. Cut away the roots and blanch the vegetable in boiling water, then dry in the sun, either spread out on baskets or hung up on a clothesline. Three or four days should be enough. The dried pak choi 白菜乾 can be stored for many months. Before using, soak in cold water for an hour.

Pak choi is one of the easiest of the winter vegetables to grow. The seeds are sown from September through January. They may be sown evenly directly in its growing site. The seeds germinate within five days and thinning should begin as soon as the plants start to crowd together. The thinnings can be used at the table. Continue thinning until the individual plants are about 10 cm apart when they can be left to grow to full size in six to eight weeks.

Alternatively sow the seeds in pans and transplant the seedlings into rows when they are 5 cm tall. Aphids may be a problem in warmer weather.

PAPAYA (Paw paw) 木瓜 | *Carica papaya*

This versatile succulent fruit, ubiquitous in the tropics, is a true favourite of mine. Originating in Central and South America, it is now grown throughout the tropics. It is a short-lived, fast-growing, soft-wooded large herb growing to tree size. Its trunk is unbranched unless previously damaged and shows characteristic crescentic markings from scars left by the fallen leaves. The large leaves are deeply lobed to resemble a snowflake and are carried on long petioles emerging directly from the trunk. The flowers are creamy white, waxy with a light fragrance. A white sticky latex exudes from any damaged part of the tree. Each tree may carry flowers that are exclusively female or exclusively male, though a good many would have bi-sexual or "perfect" flowers. Female flowers appear singly in the leaf axils and almost all will result in a fruit. The male tree produces masses of smaller flowers in long-stalked panicles and may produce small elongated fruit of poor quality. For this reason, a male tree is usually disposed of as being of no use once its identity becomes evident. Not, though, if you are aware of the unusual culinary flavour of its male flowers, of which more information will be given in the recipe section.

Green papaya

Hammering in a nail

Commercial growers have tinkered heavily with the papaya's genetic code. Ever since genetically modified papaya was introduced in Hawaii to resist viral disease and to restrict its height (for easier harvesting) and size (for better marketing), the genetic makeup of most trees has become very confused as non-genetic and organic trees hybridise with the genetically modified trees. It is a bit of a lottery what will spring up from a particular seed. This is very much the case in Mainland China.

Start papaya from seed, putting four or five in a small 7-cm pot. Discard all but the strongest seedling. This will grow rapidly and outgrow its pot in about four or five weeks, reaching about 15 cm in height. It can now be transplanted to its permanent site, either in the ground or in a large container such as a dragon urn. Container-grown trees can reach a respectable size and bring forth good fruit. Papaya enjoys tropical conditions and revels in our Hong Kong summers with growth slowing down somewhat in the winter. If a tree seems to lag behind in fruit production, traditional local farmers will drive a long (and preferably rusty!) nail into the base of the trunk. This is supposed to whip the tree to greater effort in doing its job. Many years ago I had two old traditional Chinese amahs who would perform this ritual (it was pointless for me to resist for it would have been done in secret anyway) with every papaya tree that I grew. I must say, with good results! How might this apparent sabotage possibly work its paradoxical magic? One possible explanation is that stress sometimes brings out the best in trees. Perhaps this is because adverse conditions prompt the tree to sense it might soon meet its demise. It responds by doing everything possible to ensure the survival of the species, thrusting out flowers, fruits, seeds, the whole lot, in one great effort to save the race. This phenomenon affects some other trees and shrubs as well and would seem to validate Nietzsche's premise that "*that which does not kill us makes us stronger*".

Home-grown papaya is one of the best examples of how fruits raised at home beat shop-bought produce hands down. Commercial fruits are picked before maturity to ripen, often unevenly, in transit. The home gardener, on the other hand, has the luxury of allowing his fruit to ripen evenly, and to perfection on the tree. No contest. Papayas can also be used in the green state. It is shredded and eaten raw in Thai salads, or can be stir-fried or used in stews. Papaya that is partly ripened makes a superlative soup. A recipe for this will be found elsewhere in this book.

A tree may last about five years. Tall trees are very susceptible to snapping in high winds, the large leaves catching the wind like sails. To lessen this threat, consider removing some of the lower leaves with the approach of a typhoon. A tree top-heavy with fruit is particularly at risk. Be ready with available seedlings to replace your trees as required when they run out of steam.

Two medicinal properties of papaya are well-known. The green fruit contains papain, an enzyme which is effective in reducing swelling from trauma. It has sound scientific grounding and is available for this purpose from pharmacies as papain or papase tablets. This enzyme also has a certain digestive action which is put to use in the kitchen as a meat tenderiser. A thick slice of green papaya when cooked with tough cuts of meat such as brisket is very effective in softening the meat. If you do not believe this, I strongly suggest you try it! The second medicinal application is to aid digestion, and this is said to be brought about by a substance in the fruit that resembles the gastric digestive enzyme pepsin.

Papaya, pot grown

Ripe papaya

PARSNIP 歐洲蘿蔔 | *Pastinaca sativa*

Parsnip is a delicious vegetable rarely seen in Hong Kong, except occasionally in expensive supermarkets. Certainly I have never seen it growing anywhere locally, and according to S.Y. Hu's *Food Plants of China*, it is rarely grown on the mainland as well. It prefers cool weather, apparently thriving after a period of frost. In addition, it is usually described as having a relatively long growing period, though in my local experience it is ready for harvesting in only three to four months.

It is a biennial root vegetable, grown as an annual. Parsnip is much like its relative the carrot, which it closely resembles, except for its cream colour and a significantly longer, tapering root. This root, commonly 20 cm in length requires loose, deep soil, free of stones. However, its cultivation is straightforward, despite our frost-free winters, needing very little attention and is seldom troubled by disease or pests.

Sow the seeds where they are to grow in late October. Germination takes 10–14 days. As the seedings begin to crowd, thin out 10 cm apart. Harvest when the leaves begin to yellow. Pull the plant carefully, digging around the root so as not to snap the tip. Parsnip has pale yellow flesh with a distinctive, sweet taste and smell, excellent for soups, stews or purées. It deserves greater recognition and I would like to see it more widely cultivated.

Parsnip

PEANUT (Groundnut) 花生 | *Arachis hypogaea*

Peanut is a native of South America which is now widely grown all over the world as an important commercial crop. It is arguably the world's favourite snack, rendered in many forms. An important source of cooking oil and peanut butter, it also provides dense calories in energy-rich food supplements. As a legume, peanut fixes nitrogen from the air and deposits it in its roots. This is the reason why it can be used as "green manure"—to be grown and then dug into the ground to enrich the soil.

Although called a nut, peanut being a legume, is actually a pulse. It has pinnate leaves with a variable number of leaflets and small yellow flowers. As the flower fades the stalk or "peg" lengthens and curves downwards towards the ground for the pod to develop under the surface (*hypogaea* means "under the earth") where within the shell, one to four seeds develop. Harvest by digging up the whole plant, like potatoes.

Peanut showing "pegs"

Harvested peanuts

Peanut is not a plant commonly grown in home gardens but I grow it all the time because of its very interesting growth pattern. Visitors to my garden are always amazed when I demonstrate how the pods develop beneath the surface.

Grow peanuts by buying fresh peanuts from a Chinese grocery and plant them straight into the ground, much as you would plant beans. Start sowing in February and harvest eight to ten weeks later. The plants self-seed, and you will find little plantlets appearing all over the area. In fact they can be grown throughout the year.

Peanut is a good source of vitamin E, folate and niacin. It also has as much antioxidant as most fruits and is therefore cardio-protective. The oil is rich in monounsaturated fats, also cardio-protective. One problem with peanut is the occasional allergic reaction to it. The reaction varies in severity, but at worst, it may result in anaphylactic shock which may be fatal. About 1–2% of the population of North America is affected, but it seems to be much less of a problem in Asia. Nevertheless, food containing peanut must always be labelled to indicate its presence.

PINEAPPLE 菠蘿 | *Ananas comosus*

You are unlikely to save much on your bill for fruits if you grow pineapple, but it is an interesting novelty plant that is easy for an urban gardener to grow. The plant itself is quite dramatic and holds its own as an ornamental.

When this South American bromeliad was first introduced into Europe as a rare exotic, it was a great compliment for a guest to be invited to partake of it. Hence the use of pineapple motifs in the architecture of Europe to symbolise hospitality. Extensively grown in the tropics, pineapples were once commercially farmed in the New Territories and on Lantau Island. Between raising pineapples and raising concrete high-rises, it is not difficult to understand which of the two prevailed. Supplies now come mainly from the Philippines and China.

The pineapple plant is a perennial herb with tough, pointed, grey-green, strap-shaped leaves arranged in a dense rosette, bromeliad-fashion. The edges of the leaves are spiny and can deliver a nasty cut if handled roughly. A short flowering stem bears up to 200 flowers arranged in a mosaic. This is topped by the characteristic crown of leaves. The resulting fruits eventually coalesce to form the complete pineapple.

In farms, pineapples are propagated by detaching slips or shoots from the base of the plants. The city gardener, having no access to these shoots, can just as easily raise a pineapple by detaching the rosette of leaves on the crown of a shop-bought fruit and planting this in a 30-cm pot of ordinary garden soil. Very little attention needs to be given to the plant, but the growing period is long, from 8–12 months, before you can proudly harvest and display your home-grown pineapple.

Pineapple flower stalk

Pineapple flowers

Pineapple fruit

Ready to eat

POMELO 柚子 | *Citrus maxima*

Pomelo flowers

The pomelo is a native of Malaysia and Thailand but is now grown all over Southeast Asia and tropical areas around the world. It is the largest of the citrus fruits, reaching 1 kg or more in weight. The rind is very thick and slightly spongy, enclosing flesh that may be white, yellow or pink. Its taste is reminiscent of grapefruit but sweeter and without its bitterness.

The tree, which may reach 10 m in height, is very common in Hong Kong especially in rural villages, but is also found growing wild in the countryside. The young branches are flat, ridged and angled, armed with long and fearsome spines. Cream-coloured flowers develop in March, usually announcing their presence with a delicious fragrance even before the flowers are easily visible. Fruit may be picked in October or November but fruiting is often in cycles, with good and bad years.

Pomelo

Should the city gardener want to grow this tree it is best to buy a young sapling from a nursery or from the Mong Kok flower market. My own tree has an interesting history. My late mother planted a seed many years ago without any great expectations. I now have a tree 4 m tall, in the best of health growing in a planter.

Pomelo is an extremely popular fruit in Hong Kong. In our markets, pomelos may be green and round, usually from Thailand, or yellow and pear-shaped, usually from China. Picked fruit can be stored for weeks without spoiling and some believe the quality improves after a period of storage. The rind is very useful. It can be candied, pickled or eaten as a savoury in Chinese cooking. The leaves are highly aromatic when crushed, and are sold in markets, especially around Chinese New Year time to perfume bath water and for detoxification.

POTATO 薯仔 | *Solanum tuberosum*

Potato flowers

Many of my friends are surprised when they find potatoes in my garden. Most people associate potatoes with a huge field and not a container. Not necessarily so.

Solanum is a very large genus of over a thousand species that includes trees, climbers, perennials and annuals. It includes important vegetables such as the potato and the eggplant though some species are deadly poisonous. Native to South America, potato is the most widely eaten vegetable in western countries and is a staple source of starch. It is a tuberous-rooted perennial grown as an annual for its edible tubers.

Potatoes, the harvest

Although potatoes can be grown from seeds, it is almost impossible to find these seeds and, besides, it is not the preferred method. Good results from vegetative propagation using ordinary market-bought potatoes can be expected. Allow the potatoes to age in a corner of the kitchen until the "eyes" sprout. When they are about 2 cm high they can be planted out. One potato may be divided into two or more pieces as long as each piece bears an "eye". In a small garden or verandah, potatoes can be grown in large pots or urns. Another option is to use black heavy-duty rubbish bags, doubled-up. Cut a few drainage holes at the bottom and fill with ordinary garden soil—potatoes are not particular about soil. Plant the sprouts just under the soil surface. The best time to plant is October to December.

The erect stems are slightly hairy and bear large, dark green pinnate leaves with three or five pairs of heart-shaped leaflets. The flowers appear in pendant clusters of white or mauve, very similar to the flowers of eggplant. Its fruits are like green berries almost identical to wild eggplant (*S. torvum*). When the plant has mostly wilted, it is time to dig up your potatoes. But before you actually do this, gently probe under the soil surface to test the size of the tubers. If the tubers are too small, replace the soil and try again sometime later. This rubbish bag method can easily produce a yield of 1 kg or more.

PUMPKINS 南瓜類 | *Cucurbita sp.*

Female pumpkin flower

Male pumpkin flower

Pumpkins, gourds and squashes are all related and the terms are applied loosely. They are an important summer crop: all varieties grow rapidly and are great fun to cultivate. The gardener is able to choose from a wide array of shapes, sizes and colours, more varieties being introduced every year. Lately, small squat Japanese pumpkins of about 500 g are becoming very popular especially for its convenient size. My definite favourite, though, is the locally-grown elongated or pear-shaped *C. moschata* which is always available in our wet markets. Those on sale are usually about 2–3 kg but in a large garden they can grow to an enormous size, up to 10 kg. I like these best both for the ease of cultivation and for a taste I believe to be superior to other more fancy forms of *C. moschata.*

Sow the seeds in April when the weather has shown signs of warming up. Another sowing can be made in October when there is little danger of heavy rains. Those with lots of space can simply let the vine sprawl over the ground, but otherwise grow them against a support. This may be a convenient fence or wall, or a bamboo trellis of any design. The seeds are best sown where they are to grow, at the base of its support. Plant three or four seeds then keep only the strongest seedling to grow on. Male and female flowers appear, the latter easily identified by the bulbous base of the flowers. Hand-pollination is a useful, if time-consuming method of increasing the chances of fertilisation.

Japanese pumpkin

Butternut pumpkin

Flat pumpkin

Local pumpkin

When the plant has reached the top of its support it can be stopped, allowing the lateral spurs, which bear the most flowers, to develop. Once the fruit sets, the rate of growth is amazing and it is a great thrill to watch its daily progress.

Advantage can be taken of the great variation in shapes and colours by using gourds as ornaments. If used for this purpose, the fruits should be left on the vine to mature thoroughly and for the skin to harden. They should then be cut down and dried in the sun for two weeks. A coat of clear varnish will preserve the vivid colours.

RADISH 葉蘿蔔 / 蘿蔔 | *Raphanus sativa*

Radish

The red radish, with its pure white flesh and red skin, is grown as a salad root vegetable, eaten raw and valued for its sharp, peppery taste. The root, which appears partly above ground, is globular although some varieties such as "French Breakfast" have elongated roots with white tips. It has no place in local Chinese cooking. Radish is one of the quickest crops from sowing to harvest: just four or five weeks. This makes it a very good choice for teaching children about gardening—sure and rapid success and an attractive result.

Start the plants in September through December. If grown in the ground, prepare trenches 5 cm deep. Sow the seeds thinly and cover with a fine layer of soil. As the seedlings grow, fill in the trenches from the sides to give the leggy plants some lateral support. Thin out to 5 cm apart. Radish can just as easily be grown in 22-cm pots. The radishes are ready for pulling when about 3 cm in diameter.

Far more highly prized in Hong Kong than the red radish is the white radish *Raphanus sativa* var. *longipinnatus* 蘿蔔. It is equally or even more important in Japan where it is known as daikon. It would be inconceivable to imagine Japanese cooking without daikon which is prepared in dozens of ways. White radish is used in soups, stews and to make the famous radish pudding loh pak koh 蘿蔔糕 which is universally loved. It is also used in pickles.

Start the plants in October. Every year my seedman reminds me not to plant before 24 October. Even though there seems to be some magic about that date, I usually plant around mid-October. A second sowing for succession can be made in January. The ground needs to be properly prepared, dug thoroughly and cleared of stones. Dig in some good compost to ensure good drainage. Prepare little holes in the ground 7 cm deep and at least 20 cm apart each way. Sow four seeds into each hole and cover with 1 cm of soil. Germination takes only three or four days. As the seedlings grow taller, choose the most vigorous to grow on and thin out the rest. Fill in the holes from time to time to prevent the seedlings from toppling over. Growth is very brisk and luxuriant foliage soon breaks forth. The basal, pinnatifid leaves are rough and slightly hairy, and may reach 60 cm in length. If the plants are grown close together, remove the lower leaves as they turn yellow. This will open up more space and let in light. The pure white roots grow plump and long—up to 40 cm and may reach 2 kg or more each.

Even with well prepared soil, the root tends to raise itself partly to above ground level. Harvest in 60–70 days. This is one crop I would not recommend for pots.

One smaller variety of white radish 冬瓜蘿蔔 can be started in July or August. This does not reach the quality of the winter radish but again, it is an easily grown, early harvested crop. Remember to ask for the correct seed for the season. A slower growing green radish 青蘿蔔 is also easy to grow but usually does not grow longer than 25 cm. Recently I have also seen a variety with pinkish skin and flesh but I have no experience of growing it.

I am sometimes asked by passers-by if I could spare them some of the radish leaves. Apparently they are sought after for herbal medication said to be for cancer prevention.

Misty the cat and white radish

Hamlet the guinea pig inspects summer white radish

White radish

Rice

RICE 稻 | *Oryza sativa*

粒粒皆辛苦 This Chinese aphorism translates as "every grain of rice comes from hard labour". I grew rice to prove this to myself, and in doing so was greatly humbled. How immense the value of rice, yet how little we respect it as we waste tonnes of it every day. How painful to see mounds of uneaten rice slopped into the rubbish bin in every eating establishment, even the meanest of them all. How do we stop this waste? Rice is the most important staple food in the world and has been grown for 10,000 years. It is grown in flooded fields with two crops a year in Southern China, following sowings in the second and the sixth months of the lunar calendar. According to the International Grains Council, the world's rice output for the year 2013-2014 was 478 million tonnes, the biggest producer being China. However, even the 200 million tonnes produced by China is not sufficient to feed the country and it has now become a net importer of rice.

Rice, the harvest

The origin of domesticated rice has been a subject of fierce debate for a very long time. It has been uncertain whether domestication took place at a single location or independently at several locations. Proponents of the single location theory have marginally favoured India over China as that site. That is, until very recently. Several research centres in the United States conducted tests using modern techniques of computer algorithms and studies of gene fragments from various wild and domesticated rice species, and came to the conclusion that rice was first domesticated in China, in the Yangtze River valley. Using a unique reverse "molecular clock" in rice genes, the researchers determined that domesticated rice first appeared between 8,200 and 13,500 years ago. This is in agreement with earlier archaeological evidence of domesticated rice production, storage and cooking in the Yangtze valley 10,000 years ago. These important findings have been reported online ahead of print on 2 May, 2011 in the *Proceedings of the National Academy of Sciences of the United States of America*. The debate is not likely to end here so do not adjust your set.

What I grew was only in a large container, steeped in water. My harvest was a mere handful of rice grains and had I been able to husk the grains—which I was not—it would have provided me with a mere half bowlful of rice when cooked.

I planted the seeds in early April, as the Indian cuckoo on the wing called out 早插早熟 "sow early, reap early". The container was kept standing in a tray of water which was kept filled until the rice grains formed, after which it was left to dry.

Why not give it a try? You will never take a grain of rice for granted again. Help stop the waste.

SPINACH 波菜 | *Spinacia oleracea*

Spinach was first recorded in China in the 7th century. It is an annual grown for its tender, rich-green leaves which are entire or dentately lobed. Picked young, the leaves are delicious in salads. Mature plants may reach 30 cm and are eaten cooked. The roots are conical with red coloration at the top. Although the plant is sold whole, roots and all, I only pick the leaves as they are needed and by so doing extend the production life of the plant.

I had great trouble growing spinach successfully in my roadside vegetable plot. The plants bolted early and were useless for eating. It was not until one of my neighbours, a professional seed dealer, pointed out the overhead street lights to me. Spinach is a cool season short-day crop and the extension of the day from the street lights was the problem. I have taken to growing spinach, now with success, in pots located on my verandah, away from the glare of the street lights.

The seeds are sown, after soaking in water for a day, from October through January. Patience is needed as it may take ten days or more for germination to take place. Spread the seeds evenly where they are to grow as the seedlings do not take kindly to transplantation. Thin the seedlings as necessary to prevent crowding, then pick the leaves as they are needed when mature.

Spinach ranks high among vegetables in nutritional value. The comic strip *Popeye* made extravagant claims to its strength-giving properties ("I fight to the finish 'cos I eat my spinach!"), but hopefully may have persuaded some readers to increase the consumption of vegetables in general. Spinach has high vitamin and antioxidant content. Vitamin K is especially well represented and this has led to the advice that people on the anticoagulant warfarin should avoid excessive consumption of spinach. Vitamin K is an antidote to warfarin and will diminish its therapeutic effect.

Oxalic acid is also present in significant amounts and spinach consumption again should be limited in those patients who suffer from a rare form of kidney stones that are composed of oxalic acid.

Spinach

SQUASHES AND MELONS 瓜類

As mentioned earlier, squashes, pumpkins, melons and gourds are very similar and the terms are often interchangeable. Because their cultivation is very similar, a number of different plants will be grouped together in this section. All are easy to grow and are climbing plants needing some support either from fences or trellises. They are warm season crops, started when the weather begins to warm up in March or April.

Prepare the supports. This depends very much on what you have available. A lot of my squashes are grown on fences: they are ready-made and sturdy but they need to be in a position of adequate sun. Bamboo canes can be used to build any form of trellis that pleases you. Then plant three or four seeds at the base of the supports in holes 2 cm deep. As most of these seeds are quite large, the seedlings are correspondingly large and appear early, in four to five days. Alternatively, sow the seeds in 12-cm pots to be planted out later, for reasons discussed in the earlier section on "Sowing". The plants should be stopped when they reach the top of their supports in order to allow the flower-bearing laterals greater freedom to develop. All have distinct male and female flowers, the latter being those with the swollen ovary at the base. All benefit from hand pollination if you have the time on your hands. Young plants should receive a first feeding with a liquid fertiliser when they show an early growth spurt. Thereafter restrict feeding until the flowers appear, then feed with liquid fertiliser or organic pellets every two weeks. Squashes should be picked before full maturity for good eating quality, but some varieties should be ripened on the vine and some have special uses if allowed to mature as will be mentioned below.

All squashes have a terrible enemy in the fruit fly which targets the fruit just as it develops after fertilisation. Inflicting a single needling wound is all it takes to bring about the demise of the fruit. Counter this problem by deploying sticky traps or provide some physical barrier such as paper bags to ward them off.

Bitter Squash (Bitter melon, Karela) 苦瓜 | *Momordica charantia*

This squash has a decidedly bitter taste and may therefore not have universal appeal. Nonetheless, it is an important vegetable all over Asia, eaten cooked in many ways, often combined with various meats. The bitter taste, if found to be too strong, can be tempered by briefly blanching the squash in salted water.

Bitter squash

Bitter squash is an oval fruit tapering at the tip, with a unique appearance. It has several irregular longitudinal ridges separated by a very knobbly surface. In recent years new cultivars with variations in colour and form have entered the market. Some of the new forms are less bitter. The vine has delicate-looking, palm-like leaves, deeply lobed. It climbs by non-branching tendrils.

Bitter squash

As with most bitter vegetables, bitter squash has been used in traditional medicine for problems of digestion and flatulence. Like most plants used as herbs, varied and fanciful claims are made of its healing properties. One claim that is not fanciful and has been shown in medical research to be authentic is that bitter melon can reduce blood sugar levels. This has led it to be hailed as a treatment for diabetes. Note, though, that one would need to ingest approximately 5 kg of bitter melon every day in order to achieve a therapeutic dose!

Bottle squash

Bottle squash 葫蘆瓜 | *Lagenaria siceraria*

I grow bottle squash more as a novelty than as a preferred vegetable for the table. It is elegant to look at but is fairly bland when cooked for food. It is grown exactly like the rest of the squashes in this section. The light green squash or gourd is markedly waisted at the centre, slimmer above and bulbous below. If left to grow to old age it develops a hard skin that can keep its shape and appearance for many months—useful as an ornament.

Cantaloupe (Rock melon, Musk melon) 蜜瓜 | *Cucumis melo*

A home-grown cantaloupe is a delicious desert fruit that is well worth growing in the summer. I have always grown them in large 30-cm pots with light support from a few bamboo canes. If these canes can rest against a fence, so much the better. Growing them in pots has the great advantage that they can be moved away when heavy rains or typhoons threaten.

Cantaloupe

Prepare the pots with good drainage, lining the bottom with crock or polystyrene foam chunks, then fill with earth mixed with a handful of organic fertiliser pellets. Plant four seeds in each pot, eventually selecting a single plant to grow on. Male and female flowers are easily recognised and hand-pollination should be carried out. Keep well watered and mulched. Allow no more than two (sometimes even one) fruit to develop on each plant. Reluctant as you may be, eliminate any extra young fruit and pinch out the leading shoot. Fruit flies will threaten: wrap up your precious crop with a paper bag or something similar. Marvel as the melons develop to twice the size of your fist before testing to see if it is ripe for picking. Do this by sniffing the blossom end of the fruit: it should give off a flowery aroma. If pressing on this spot also reveals a slight "give", then your fruit is ready for you to enjoy.

Chanterais

There are numerous other varieties of *C. melo*. Some, like the cantaloupe have a ribbed and netted rind with orange flesh, while others, like the honeydew melon have smooth skins and pale green flesh. There are too many to describe individually. All are heat-loving and are great summer crops.

Hairy squash 節瓜 | *Benincasa hispida* var. *chiehquah*

This very tasty summer vegetable grows on a medium-sized, vigorous vine. It is grown for its cylindrical succulent fruit which is covered with fine hairs throughout ("hispida" means "hairy"). I consider this to be the most important of the summer squashes. It can be stir-fried, stuffed or used in soup.

Hairy squash

Start the seeds in late March or April in the ground or in a large container at the base of a chosen support. The leaves are dentate 5–7 lobes, covered with fine hairs. The squash should be picked when young, 10–20 cm long, and still covered throughout with hairs, preferably with the withered bloom attached. If left on the vine to mature, the fruit can grow to an enormous size, losing its hairs and becoming covered with a light white bloom. When it reaches this stage, at 5–7 kg, it becomes very much like winter melon, described below, and can be used in the kitchen in exactly the same way. After picking, the mature squash can be kept up to two months at room temperature without much deterioration.

Silk squash (Angled loofah, Patola) 絲瓜
Luffa acutangula

This is a long, slender squash, mildly club-shaped at the end, with distinctive longitudinal ridges along its length. This is a tasty squash, eaten cooked with the skin lightly peeled, leaving some green to retain its ridges and a pleasing colour.

Silk squash: note the fly paper

It is grown as a warm season vegetable, started in March or April, but it also succeeds admirably with a late sowing at the end of August. This later sowing should produce a crop before the onset of short days and long nights as the weather cools down.

Mature "loofah"

The commercial product

Soak the seeds in water for one day before sowing. The squash grows to about 60 cm long but becomes very fibrous if left on the vine to fully mature. Holding the thin end of the squash in your hand, it should show a decided flexibility which is lost when it is too old.

A closely related variety, *Luffa aegyptiaca*, is more fleshy and not ridged although it may be slightly grooved. Left on the vine to mature, its extensive vascular system develops into a dense network of fibres forming a sponge-like structure. This is used commercially as "loofah" or "luffa" to be used as a bath sponge or for general scrubbing duties in the kitchen. The young fruit may be eaten in the same way as *L. acutangula*.

Vegetable marrow (Zucchini) 美洲南瓜 | *Cucurbita pepo*

Zucchini

Vegetable marrow

This is included here because again its cultivation is so similar to the other squashes and melons. However, besides growing as a summer crop, it can also be started in the autumn. Vegetable marrow has long been ignored by local farmers, but is gaining popularity notably in organic farms that have been springing up recently. Locally, it is sometimes referred to as "jade squash" 翠玉瓜. Basically there are two types, the trailing and the bush types. I always stay with the bush type because it requires little support if any, and is much more compact in size. The trailing type is very similar in cultivation to, say, hairy squash. The fruit should be picked at about 15 cm when tender and juicy. Increasingly the smaller zucchini varieties—which are harvested when immature—are gaining popularity and these are great eaten raw in salads, or as a cooked vegetable.

Watermelon 西瓜 | *Citrullus lunatus*

There are over a hundred varieties of watermelon varying from a half to a hundred kilograms in size. The most widely sold fruits are the seedless melons of which China is the world's biggest producer. Enjoyed as a fruit or juiced, few know that even the rind is edible, as a vegetable or, more frequently, pickled.

The larger varieties are prostrate vines grown to sprawl over the ground, but the miniature varieties can be grown even in a verandah in a 23-cm pot with some support. These small melons are the only ones I have attempted and found quite simple to grow.

Watermelon

Winter melon (Wax gourd) 冬瓜 | *Benincasa hispida*

This is probably the largest of all fruiting vegetable crops. Basically it is a very large version of hairy squash that grows on a very large vine. The melon develops a thick, hairless, waxy skin and may reach 20 kg in weight if given enough space to flex its muscles. Its size makes it difficult to grow except in larger gardens. It can be attempted in dragon urns but expect a correspondingly abridged harvest. It needs a really solid trellis and the developing fruit needs to be netted and tied to support in order to prevent it from falling under its own weight. If space is not a limiting factor, simply let it grow on the ground—there are fewer problems that way.

Winter melon

A favourite way of enjoying winter melon is in a soup, mixed with diced pork, Chinese ham and conpoy. An even more special way to prepare the soup is to use the whole melon (with the top sliced off) as the receptacle for cooking the soup in a steamer 冬瓜盅. This is a job that might defeat most home cooks but is a favourite restaurant staple.

STRAWBERRY 草莓 | *Fragaria*

For many years in Hong Kong, strawberries were regarded as something of a luxury, imported from far away, expensive and aristocratic—think strawberries and cream, with champagne. This is no longer the case, as supplies increase, and producers now moving closer to home, in Asia. Locally produced strawberries are still not generally available, but specialist organic farms are now springing up, supplying mostly up-market establishments for the present.

There are about a dozen species of this genus, native to the temperate areas of the northern hemisphere. They are perennials with a low-growing habit, tufted or creeping. The distinctive palmate leaves are composed of three toothed leaflets and the flowers are white with five petals, appearing in cymes. The fruit itself is actually a false fruit, made up of tiny pips on a fleshy receptacle.

The small-time Hong Kong gardener would do best to start off with young plants purchased from a nursery. These are available in late October and can often be found in the Mong Kok flower market. The plants are best grown in rectangular plastic containers raised off the ground—hanging from a fence or railing, or propped up on bricks. The plants themselves should be positioned at the margin of the planter so that when the fruits form, they will hang over the edge, away from the soil surface. A delightful crop of ripe strawberries should be ready for picking in about two months—a good way to impress your friends!

After fruiting, the plants can be kept so that runners are produced which are used for propagation the following season. These runners are pegged down onto small pots containing potting soil and little plants will develop in due course. If this is too much of a chore, then start with new, bought plants again. Strawberries can also be started from seed—indeed some species produce no runners and must be so started—but this is even more of a chore.

Strawberry - propagation by runners

Young strawberry

The harvest

SUGAR CANE 甘蔗 | *Saccharum officinarum*

I found the following passage in the Catholic Bible referring to natural medicines from the earth: "*did not a piece of wood once sweeten the water*" (Ecclesiasticus/Sirach 38:5). I wonder, could this be a reference to sugar cane? Another reference came from the ancient Persians who first encountered sugar cane on their arrival in India around the fifth century BC. They described it as "a reed that makes honey without bees".

Sugar cane is a tall, robust perennial grass grown in all tropical regions of the globe for the production of sugar. It has also become an important source of biofuel. In Brazil, there are no longer any light vehicles running on petrol as all have switched to ethanol produced from sugar cane. Sceptics decry the shunting of a food source to industry and also claim that Brazil is the only country capable of a sustainable biofuel industry because of the huge tracts of land available for agriculture.

Sugar cane is easily raised from 20 cm long cuttings, either laid on its side or inserted half into the ground at a 45° angle. Cuttings are usually successful although patience is required as it may be two or three months before they take. The dark purple jointed stems grow to 3 m tall with the base reaching 6 cm in diameter. A slimmer variety with greenish yellow stems is also commonly cultivated. The long flat leaves are extremely sharp at the edges and special care is needed in handling them to avoid a nasty cut. I speak from experience. As the leaves dry and fade, they should be removed. Failure to do so encourages ants to nest and new growth to sprout from the protected nodes. This diverts energy from the growing stem. Attention must also be paid to the very numerous new canes that sprout from the base. Most of them should be rubbed out, leaving only a limited number to grow on to full size.

I am told by many local gardeners that to maintain good production the sugar cane plant should be dug up and replaced every two or three years. I have never followed this advice and have no reason to regret it as my sugar cane keeps growing lustily without any such measures.

Sugar cane stems are passed through metal rollers to extract its juice which is enjoyed unalloyed as a healthful drink. The juice contains at least 15% natural sugars. The home gardener is not likely to have a metal press available, but an easily prepared sugar cane drink is recommended and referred to in the section on recipes.

In traditional medicine sugar cane is said to have a cooling and diuretic effect. All other claims are probably apocryphal.

It should also be remembered that excessive sugar consumption is one of the main causes of obesity. Much of this excess sugar is consumed hidden in sweet beverages, fruit juices and confectionery.

Sugar cane

SWEET CORN (Maize) 粟米 | *Zea mays*

Ripening sweet corn

Sweet corn "Super Sweet"

Baby corn

If ever you find a difference between shop-bought vegetables and those you grew yourself, you will find it especially in sweet corn. The sugar content of corn begins to fall as soon as it is picked and taste suffers as a result.

Sweet corn is native to Central America and was first grown by American Indians. It was introduced to European settlers in the late 18th century by the Iroquois tribe and its popularity rapidly spread. Sweet corn is harvested when the kernels are plump and juicy and eaten as a vegetable. This differs from field corn (of which sweet corn is a genetic variation) which is picked when the kernels are dry and treated as a grain. In Taiwan a new strain has been developed known as "baby corn", which is a miniature corn picked before the kernels develop and designed especially for canning. Seeds of this type are now appearing in seed shops.

Corn is a tall grass that can be started from March or August. I tend to favour an early start so that the crop matures before the onset of the typhoon season. The seeds can be planted where they are to grow or can be started in small pots. The latter is my preferred method so as to be able to protect the seedlings in case of heavy rain. The seedlings should be ready for planting out in about three weeks. The home gardener may also grow corn in large containers and for this purpose seek out the shorter varieties such as "Super Sweet" which does, in fact, live up to its name! This variety usually has mixed yellow and white kernels. Other types may be all yellow or all white, such as glutinous or "sticky" corn. Some native Indian types have an attractive mix of colours, including purple, brown and black. Female flowers appear from the lower leaf axils and are enclosed in an elongated sheath of overlapping layers of bracts. Silky, thread-like tassels emerge from the upper end when the plants are ready for pollination. Male flowers are borne on the same plant and form a plume-shaped panicle at the top of the stem. Pollen is shed and carried to the female flowers by gravity, assisted by wind. Harvest the cobs when the kernels have developed to the top or nearly the top of the cob. The cobs can be inspected from time to time by pulling back the bracts. If the kernels look full and feel like they are springy, that is the time to pick them. If they are deemed not yet ready, carefully replace the bracts and come back another day.

After the ripened cobs have been harvested, there may still be a few remnant immature cobs left on the plant. These need not be discarded with the spent plant. Instead, these immature cobs can be picked and used whole as a vegetable in the same way as the Taiwan "baby corn" mentioned above.

Several gardener friends complain to me that the corn they grow is of poor quality for having very few kernels on the cob. This is a problem for small gardens which only support a few plants, resulting in poor pollination. Counter this by keeping the plants close together, for example by planting in blocks rather than rows. After the flowers appear, shaking the plants from time to time to release a shower of pollen also helps.

SWEET POTATO 番薯 | *Ipomoea batatas*

Sweet potato shoots

Digging up

The crop

The sweet potato is often regarded as a lower-ranking crop: fed to pigs, grown when none other is available or the soil is too poor to support more valuable vegetables. Paradoxically, herein lies its strengths. Many survivors of wars and famines owe their lives to this tough, undemanding source of high quality starch and vitamins. Apart from the tubers, the shoots and leaves can be eaten and little is left to waste. Sweet potato is exceptionally nutritious, with a high calorific value, high quality protein, and a large content of vitamins. As a result, sweet potato, previously looked down upon, is now enjoying a surge of popularity in health-conscious circles. No seeds are needed; all that is required to start it off is a small piece of the tuber, tip cuttings, or any cutting with one or two nodes. Grown in ditches, vacant lots or scattered patches of soil, the sweet potato has saved many lives.

This is a sprawling, trailing plant that spreads quickly, and can be used as ground cover. The leaves may be heart-shaped or arrow-shaped, with branchlets rooting at the nodes. The flower is pink or mauve with a deeper hue at the throat. It is immediately recognisable as a close relative of the ubiquitous morning glory. The swollen tubers are fusiform, with white, yellow or purple flesh. It is rich in starch which on storing, turns to sugar, a fact made known to me from two sources: the celebrated Professor S.Y. Hu in her book *Food Plants of China*, and my quietly observant Filipina helper Cynthia. The sweet potato therefore should be eaten only after a period of storage.

Sweet potato can be grown throughout the year and I have some in my garden at all times. I grow it in a very restricted space, a very narrow planter 12.5 cm wide and 20 cm deep, within the perimeter wall of my garden. When we first moved in many years ago it supported a few asthmatic shrubs and rank weeds. Most people expect sweet potato to require deep soil and wide spaces and are genuinely surprised to see me digging out good-sized tubers up to 20 cm long, though they may be faceted from being squashed against the narrow walls.

Start your plants by buying a tuber, selecting one with flesh the colour of your choice. Keep in a warm shady place until the eyes develop into sprouts or "slips". When these reach about 2 cm high, divide the tuber into two or three pieces, each containing one or more slips. Bury these just under the surface of the soil. Keep the soil moist and Nature will do the rest. Little feeding is needed and the tubers should be ready in three or four months.

Sweet potato has an unusually interesting history especially in relation to Hong Kong and Macao, and to the spread of Christianity into China. Native to the northwestern parts of South America, where archaeological remains date to 8000 BC, domestication probably started about 4500 BC. Recently, while reading about the early settlement of Macao, I learned that the sweet potato may have spread from Brazil to mother Portugal through Portuguese maritime activity in the 16th century. It is said that every Portuguese sailing vessel at that time carried an ample supply of sweet potatoes. When a settlement was established in Macao in 1557, sweet potatoes were cultivated there and then presumably spread north into the Chinese hinterland (Source: *The Portuguese in Hong Kong and China—their beginning, settlement and progress to 1949* Vol 1, J.P. Braga, revised 2013).

The connection continues with Xu Guangqi 徐光啟, the Ming dynasty polymath. Xu Guangqi was a patriot, scholar-bureaucrat, mathematician, military expert, astronomer and agricultural scientist, to name a few of his occupations. He became greatly interested in European technology and culture through his close association with the Italian Jesuit missionaries Matteo Ricci and Sabatino de Ursis. Xu, who became one of the earliest Chinese converts to Christianity, wrote one of the first comprehensive treatises on agriculture and experimented with many new crops, and is credited with the promotion and widespread cultivation of the sweet potato in China.

Purple and yellow sweet potatoes

TARO 芋 | *Colocasia esculenta*

Taro plant

This perennial member of the Arum family is a native of tropical Asia, probably originating from Indo-Malaya. It is grown for its delicious corms which vary greatly in size. The plant grows in paddy fields and swampy muddy areas, which makes it slightly difficult for the home gardener unless you remember to keep it well watered. The leaves are large, heart-shaped carried on petioles 50–70 cm long. Taro rarely flowers as the plants have been vegetatively propagated for centuries. The corms are covered with brown fibrous scales and the slimy flesh is white with highlights of purple.

The raw corm is toxic to eat due to its content of calcium oxalate crystals, which can be eliminated by cooking. In Hong Kong it is a popular food and is sold either in the small form, the size of an egg, or a larger version up to 2 kg or more. It is sought after in the Chinese New Year season to make a savoury pudding very similar to the well-known white radish pudding. Another seasonal delicacy "taro shrimps" 芋蝦 is prepared by shredding the taro, dusting it with glutinous rice flour and deep frying the shreds which are first made up into a loose ball. This is a delicate process and is steadily becoming a lost art. Boiled taro is a staple food in the South Pacific where even the leaves are cooked as a vegetable. Taro paste, allowed to ferment, is the well-known "poi" of the Hawaiian islands. The leaf petioles have a further use—they can be salted and eaten as a pickle.

Taro

I have only attempted growing the small corms—the larger type has a long growing period and needs very boggy soil. These small corms can be found in wet markets in September when they are bought as a Mid-Autumn Festival delicacy. The corms are boiled, peeled and then eaten either with a touch of sugar or as a savoury snack dipped in soy sauce. Do not forget to buy a few extra corms to plant. Bury them 5 cm below the surface—they grow very easily if provided with plenty of water.

TOMATO 蕃茄 | *Solanum lycopersicon* syn. *Lycopersicon esculentum*

Readers will find that both scientific names for tomato are in common use, although ge evidence suggests the former is the more correct. Academic debate on this subject conti

Seemingly every beginner at vegetable gardening would first think of planting toma It must be the all-time favourite vegetable. To me, there is nothing more evocative o gardening spirit than the smell of a crushed tomato leaf. It simply spurs me on to rush out garden and get growing!

The tomato comes from Central America and was cultivated by the Incas in Peru and Ecu and the Aztecs in Mexico at the time of the Spanish conquest. However, the tomato was a regarded with suspicion by the Europeans and it was not until the late 19th century that it g worldwide acceptance as a food plant. The tomato was also known as "love apple" for its sup aphrodisiac properties. I invite you to reach your own conclusions on this point.

This soft-stemmed plant has deeply lobed leaves and grows up to 2 m. The flowe yellow and the soft, succulent fruit mostly red or yellow though some varieties have un colouration. The gardener has the pleasant task of choosing exactly what tomato to grow a giddy list of available plant configurations, as well as fruit size, shape and colour. I like something new every year, although I do have my favourites.

Any tomato can be grown in containers of an appropriate size. Tall tomatoes will n 23-cm pot and some kind of staking or support. Dwarf plants such as "Tiny Tim" need c 12-cm pot and being of a bushy habit, need no support at all. "Tiny Tim" would be an exc choice for window-sill gardeners. I hesitate to recommend what others to choose, but of c it would depend on what is available for you to buy. Some popular tomatoes are "Beefs extra-large fruit with prominent ribbing; "Roma", pear-shaped and especially good for s

Beefsteak

"Speckled Roman" striped tomato

and canning; and "Moneymaker", a heavy cropper. In recent years I have enjoyed success with various forms of "black" tomatoes. Some of these are indeed jet black, others merely a dusky red or mahogany colour: most are very good to eat. I have also enjoyed growing a heritage Italian variety Costoluto (meaning "ribbed") fiorentino, a seductively shaped, heavily-ribbed tomato.

Costoluto fiorentino

Hybrid F1 seeds are expensive to buy, but the chances of a good harvest of perfect fruit is very high. I have tried "Grenadier" and "Shirley" with equal success but there are many others. Hybrids are designed for commerce: you cannot save the seeds and new seeds need to be bought every year. With the upswing of hybrids, many old varieties, as much as 50%, have been lost forever. Fortunately, a renewed interest in heirloom tomatoes is making its mark. Try to search out these heirloom tomatoes and help to bring them back into circulation.

The tomato is a cool season crop which I start in September through January. After the mist starts to roll in from February onwards, growth slows down appreciably. I do not grow tomatoes in the summer at all. Sow the seeds in small pots or sectioned trays. After the second leaf has appeared, thin out all but the strongest seedling. When the young plant is 7 cm tall, plant it out in the ground or a pot, burying more than half of the stem. Tomatoes enjoy full and prolonged sunshine, certainly not less than four hours a day. As with all fruiting vegetables do not feed excessively before the flowers appear at the expense of producing more foliage than needed. As the plant grows, new shoots sprout from the leaf axils. These must be pinched out to allow the leading shoot to receive all the available nutrients. When three or four trusses have appeared, consider stopping further height by pinching out the leading shoot. Some

Pearl tomato

Black tomato

Yellow pear

Vine ripened tomatoes

Tomato "Golden Queen"

tomatoes are self-terminating and do not need to be stopped. If the trusses are heavy with fruit, they may break off unless some form of support is rigged up—tying to a stake or using a supporting net. The home gardener has the enviable advantage of picking his tomatoes when dead ripe and enjoying the fruit of his labours. Note that bland-tasting industrially produced tomatoes are often picked when still green and hard (easier for shipping) and artificially ripened by exposure to ethylene gas.

A very prevalent problem with tomatoes is infestation with the tobacco mosaic virus. I find at least some of my plants affected by it at some stage every year. There is no remedy for this, and plants so affected should be discarded as soon as recognised. Do not use the plants for compost and avoid planting tomatoes again in the same place or pot for some time.

You can save seeds from your favourite (non-hybrid) tomatoes. When you scrape away the seeds from within the tomato, the seeds will be surrounded by blobs of mucus. If left to dry in this state, the seeds will eventually become enmeshed in a gooey, damp mess and will be difficult to separate. This can be avoided if you soak the fresh seeds in water for a day. This loosens up the mucus and the seeds can then be left out to dry.

3 miniature tomatoes (from left): Black, Tiny Tim, Pearl

Few people will say that they consciously eat tomatoes for the good of their health. Nevertheless, together with olive oil, the tomato is an important component of the Mediterranean diet—a diet with a reputation for promoting good health. The active health-giving ingredient in the tomato is lycopene, an antioxidant 10 times more effective than Vitamin E. Lycopene is not destroyed by cooking and is in fact four times more bioavailable in the form of tomato paste than in raw tomatoes. A 2014 publication in the open access scientific journal *PLOS ONE* reported a reduced incidence of cardiovascular disease in a study of lycopene, most likely as a result of its protective action on the lining of blood vessels known as the endothelium.

TURNIP/RUTABAGA (Swede) 蕪菁 / 洋頭菜 | *Brassica rapa* var. *rapa*

This is a cool weather vegetable grown for its globular, white-fleshed root with a delicate mustardy taste excellent for stews. The young turnip tops can also be eaten as a vegetable. Prepare a free-draining soil with no stones. Sow the seeds in October through December in rows where they are to grow. Thin the seedlings to 15 cm each way, earthing up the plants as they grow. Two or three plants may also be raised in a 23-cm pot. They grow without much trouble and should be ready for pulling in about eight weeks. Take them when 5–6 cm in diameter while they are still tender and lack any fibre. I like "Early Purple Top" for its lovely colouration and good flavour.

Turnip "Early Purple Top"

The rutabaga or swede (for Swedish turnip) (*B. rapa* var. *napro-brassica*) is a much larger plant with yellow-fleshed roots of 500 g and more. Cultivation is similar except the need for more space.

WAMPI 黃皮 | *Clausena lansium*

The name wampi is a romanisation of the Chinese name which means "yellow skin". This is a medium-sized evergreen tree reaching about 5 m in height. It is a native of South China and is widespread in Hong Kong gardens and even in the wild. The alternate pinnate leaves have 5–9 leaflets that are wavy margined and shallowly toothed. The crushed leaves have a distinct aroma that reveals its distant relation to Citrus. In the spring, tiny flowers appear in clusters at the end of the branchlets, later developing into bunches of yellow-skinned, slightly hairy, oval fruit 1.5–2 cm in diameter. The fruits are quite showy, resembling bunches of grapes loosely hanging. The tough, highly-resinous skin can be easily peeled to expose translucent flesh surrounding one to five oblong seeds that may occupy up to 40% of the volume of the fruit. When fully ripe the flesh is pleasantly sweet, but fruit short of full ripeness has strong sour overtones, detracting from its enjoyment. The fruit is not particularly popular and many locals cannot even recognise it. It makes a seasonal appearance in the markets in the late autumn in moderate quantities.

Wampi

Wampi is readily propagated from seed, and indeed large numbers of seedlings are commonly found sprouting around the base of the tree. Small trees are easily available from nurseries.

WATERCRESS 西洋菜

Rorippa nasturtium-aquaticum syn. *Nasturtium officinale*

Watercress in a pot

My ideal garden would have a babbling brook running through it, and somewhere along its course would be a pool with watercress growing. The stuff of dreams! My garden started off with mostly concrete and the only sound of running water comes from a tap! That doesn't mean that I cannot grow watercress.

Watercress, known in Chinese as "vegetable from the western ocean", was probably introduced to China by the Portuguese who know it as agrião, and who, incidentally, were once nicknamed "devils from the western ocean". It is a marsh plant in Europe and Northern Asia and, in some places, has grown to weed proportions. It has irregular compound leaves with rounded leaflets that are dark green, sometimes with hints of bronze or purple. Ideally it should be grown in clean, slowly flowing water, started in late October from 10-cm cuttings taken from market-bought plants. The plants can also be started from seed. For the majority of gardeners, reasonable watercress can be grown in pots kept well watered. Use a plastic pot or planter with a spill tray underneath. Water frequently so that the tray is never dry. Partial sun is best. The result may surprise you.

Watercress has a distinctive peppery taste and may be eaten raw as a salad herb or cooked as a vegetable. It is superb for soup, commonly of two kinds: a quick soup in which the watercress is cooked only just beyond scalding, and a slow-cooked version, usually with a hunk of pork. A piece of dried tangerine peel may be added for a slightly more exotic taste. A third version is a cream of watercress soup with the vegetable puréed.

WATER SPINACH (Morning glory, Kangkong) 蕹菜

Ipomoea aquatica

White stemmed water spinach

In my early experience of Thai restaurants, I was intrigued with the menu item "stir-fried morning glory", expecting to be served up a dish of cooked flowers! *Ipomoea* is a large genus of 500 species all of which can lay claim to the name "morning glory". This includes such diverse members as the ubiquitous flowering tropical vines and the sweet potato.

Water spinach is a leafy green vegetable available at a time when leafy green vegetables are scarce: in the summer. It is found in two forms. The aquatic white-stemmed 白骨蕹菜/水蕹菜 (actually a light green) variety grows in water and swamps. The crisp stems are hollow and bear light green broadly ovate leaves that may have a hint of yellow. Roots appear at the nodes and the plant spreads and sprawls over a large area. It can be grown in ordinary garden soil provided attention is given to heavy watering. Even so, the plants are not as luxuriant as the aquatically grown ones. The land-grown, green-stemmed form 青骨蕹菜/旱蕹菜 is grown in ordinary soil. The stems are much slimmer as are the leaves, and the whole plant is a dark green. The eating qualities of the two are different: the white has very crunchy stems and it should not be overcooked in order to preserve some of this crunch. The green version is usually cooked to a softer consistency and has a somewhat stronger taste. Stir-fried water spinach is sometimes flavoured with fermented bean curd or shrimp paste.

The seeds are large, faceted and very hard. The seeds should be soaked for one day before sowing in order to speed up germination which should take about four days. Sow only as the weather warms up in April when there is no danger of a cold snap. Harvest the plants by cutting the stalks 5 cm from the ground, keeping the tender shoots and discarding the fibrous lower ends. Further harvests can be expected from new sprouts which, amazingly, are ready for cutting in less than two weeks. One sowing is usually all it takes to keep up the supply for the whole summer, or new plots can be raised very easily from cuttings containing one or two nodes. The plants also spread by self-layering as the rooting nodes make contact with the soil.

Green stemmed water spinach

INTERESTING PLANTS, UNUSUAL EATS

Eat me!

There is a lot more to food plants than cabbage, lettuce and tomatoes. A few less usual offerings are featured here. Some may be occasionally available in markets, some you may need to grow yourself!

CELTUCE (Stem lettuce, Asparagus lettuce) 萵苣

Lactuca sativa var. *augustana*

Celtuce

Very few of my friends or guests at table are able to identify celtuce when they first see it. It is a very interesting form of lettuce where the central stalk grows thick and fleshy, and is the part of the plant that is eaten. The leaves can be eaten as well, but being a little more coarse than the usual salad lettuces, they are better cooked. At markets it is sold with most of the leaves removed. If local wet markets do not have it, try the Thai shops. The stems are harvested when 60–80 cm high reaching a diameter of 5–6 cm at the base. The leaves never form a heart and eventually change into bracts.

Grow celtuce like lettuce, as a cool season crop. Because of the size of each plant, they need to be at least 25 cm apart. One plant to a 23-cm pot will do fine.

Now comes the best part—how to eat it? The celtuce stems must be deeply peeled to remove the fibrous skin completely. This will reduce the size of the stem considerably. It is then cut into rings or ovals and can be stir-fried with a little ginger. But my favourite method of treating celtuce is to use it as a salad. Please refer to the recipe section.

CICORIA (Chicory) 野苦萵 | *Cichorium sp.*

Endive

This is an interesting vegetable, closely related to the lettuce genus Lactuca, popular in Europe but almost unknown in Hong Kong. It has an important place in the cuisines of France, Belgium and especially Italy where it is usually eaten raw in salads. I have never seen any on sale in Hong Kong, but I have come to love it so much that I grow several varieties every year. I also provide an intermittent supply to my good friends the Italian sisters of the Canossian order.

In appearance *C. intybus* is easily mistaken for lettuce or a small cabbage. There is a huge variety of leaf forms, but most have tongue-shaped leaves emerging as basal tufts from slightly swollen taproots. The stalks and lower parts of the leaves may be hairy. Some have red or purple tones that add colour to salads. Radicchio is red-leafed with white veins and is eaten raw or grilled. In cool climates, blanched hearts or "chicons" can be obtained by the exclusion of light but this is a complicated process and not something for the home gardener. All vegetables of this genus exude a sticky white sap when broken and all have a typical slight bitter taste. The dandelion-like flowers are blue. My favourite cultivars are "Zuccerina di Trieste", "Bianca di Milano" and "Variegata di Chioggia".

Some forms of chicory are grown for their roots which, when dried and ground up, can be used as a coffee additive or substitute. This is var. *sativum*, which is of no interest to the city gardener, whereas the salad vegetables are var. *foliosum*.

Zuccerina di Trieste

Bianca di Milano

Radicchio

C. endivia (endive or scarole) is an open-hearted vegetable with elaborately cut crispy leaves that have a sharper, more bitter taste. Endive can be made to have a blanched heart—this can be done by placing a small plate over the centre for a number of days.

Cichorium is a cool season vegetable to be planted in October. I have never found any seeds on sale locally and I source mine from Italy courtesy of the Canossian sisters. It grows extremely well in Hong Kong and I am trying to interest some of the organic farms in Hong Kong to grow and market this very worthwhile crop.

DRAGON FRUIT (Night-blooming cereus, Pitaya)

火龍果 / 霸王花 | *Hylocereus undatus*

Brian van Langenberg

Dragon fruit flower

Dragon fruit is a native of Central and South America. Although a cactus, it is not found in the excessively hot and dry desert areas of those localities but rather prefers places with some shade for part of the day.

The succulent, spiny stems are three-angled, in segments of varying lengths. If given the opportunity, the plant will scramble pell-mell up trees and rough walls, assisted by fibrous aerial roots. Flowers appear in the summer, and what flowers! Exquisitely beautiful and funnel-shaped, easily 15–18 cm across and 25 cm long, the flowers are the purest white with numerous delicate stamens, slightly shorter than the style. The flowers are almost identical to those of *Epiphyllum oxypetalus* (Queen of the night) and give off a pleasing, delicate fragrance. The flowers are self-sterile, and as they open only at night—for not more than a few hours—natural pollination must depend on night-time visitors such as bats and moths. These visitors are unreliable, or may even be absent in some localities, hence hand pollination is strongly advised for better results. A toothbrush, a Q-tip or something similar can be used for the task. If pollination is successful, large, red egg-shaped fruit will result. The fruit is covered with a soft, thick skin in red or pink with numerous fleshy scales, and may weigh up to 500 g. The sweet flesh is either white

Hand pollination

Dragon fruit

Two-year-old dragon fruit plant: spot the flower bud

or deep red, embedded with innumerable small black seeds not unlike black sesame in appearance.

Dragon fruit is now readily available in markets and shops, although when it was first introduced some years ago, its unusual, exotic appearance was not universally appealing. Most of the fruit sold locally come from China or Southeast Asia but it is now being commercially produced in Hong Kong in a small way.

While it is possible to raise new plants from seed, it is much more practical to propagate with cuttings which usually succeed without trouble. The cuttings should be half buried or simply laid down horizontally on the soil. This is best done in the spring or early summer.

The dried flowers, known as bawang fa 霸王花, are used to brew a nourishing broth with various meats. It is believed that bawang fa has medicinal properties since the fruit has exceptionally high levels of vitamin C and antioxidants. It is also said that bawang fa may be effective in reducing blood sugar levels in diabetes.

It is interesting to note that fruits of various other cacti have been eaten in tropical and desert areas for centuries. The best example is the very common prickly pear (*Opuntia ficus-indica*) which produces, in abundance, a very delicious orange coloured fruit.

Bawang fa

HONEYSUCKLE 金銀花 | *Lonicera japonica*

This half evergreen, woody twining climber is widely grown in Hong Kong especially to clamber over fences. It has dark green ovate leaves and hairy branchlets, with two-lipped flowers that begin as white, turning yellow then dark gold at the end of the day. When in full flower in April it is a grand sight. The flowers have a delicate, exquisite fragrance best appreciated on a warm evening with light breezes.

Its flowers have many uses in traditional Chinese medicine and are included in different kinds of herbal tea, mainly for detoxification. Honeysuckle tea as a refreshing drink can be prepared by combining 2 tablespoons of dried flowers with 1 tablespoon of green tea. Add boiling water and flavour with sugar or honey to taste. It can be enjoyed either as a warm drink or iced. It has a cooling effect that counters the "heat" of fried and spicy foods.

Honeysuckle

NASTURTIUM (Indian cress) 旱金蓮 | *Tropaeolum majus*

When I serve nasturtium leaves and flowers in a salad, I often find my guests eating around them. Why? They think it is for decoration only! "Are you sure it is edible?" I quickly disabuse them of their doubts.

This is the common or garden annual nasturtium that can be grown in pots or beds. It is a tough, undemanding plant and thrives in poor soil. Excessively rich soil encourages foliage rather than flowers. This habit makes it useful as a ground cover for ugly vacant lots. It self-seeds and will come back every year—whether you like it or not! The plant has a semi-trailing habit and may climb. The round leaves are mid-green, fresh looking. Because they have a waxy covering, water collects as globules on the slightly cup-shaped leaves—a very pretty sight after a rainstorm or watering. The flowers are 5-petalled, spurred, open and trumpet-shaped with colours from a dark red through orange to a light yellow.

Although best known as an ornamental, nasturtium leaves and flowers lend an extra bite to salads. It is closely related to watercress and resembles it in its sharp, peppery taste. The flowers are also edible and make a splendid garnish for a salad that is sure to impress your guests.

Nasturtium

Many other garden flowers are edible—but that does not mean they are all good to eat. Worth trying are pansy, tuberous begonia, dandelion, snapdragon, marigold, chrysanthemum, rose and jasmine. Only eat flowers you have grown yourself or come from a known, reliable source. Never eat flowers bought from florists, nurseries or garden centres—these may have been treated with pesticides. Edible flowers may also be used to make decorative ice cubes. Place a flower at the bottom of an individual ice compartment and fill with water that has previously been boiled (to expel dissolved air) and cooled. This will ensure the cube is clear and free of air bubbles.

PAPAYA FLOWERS 木瓜花 | *Carica papaya*

Male papaya flowers

Papaya as a fruit is the product of fertilised female flowers. These are borne in the leaf axils either singly or in small clusters. The purely male tree bears instead large bunches of cream-coloured flowers borne on long stalks. Some fruits do develop, but they are small and bitter and cannot be eaten. This is why a male papaya tree is pulled up and destroyed once its sex is known. The only male papaya trees around are wild. I keep searching for them. Why is this? To me the male flowers are a rare culinary gem, something known to very few people, most of them Macanese. Please refer to the recipe section for instructions on how to prepare this delicacy.

Pumpkin flowers

PUMPKIN FLOWERS 南瓜花 | *Cucurbita sp.*

Pumpkin flower fritters

It is surprising how few people know that the flowers of pumpkins (and zucchinis and many other squashes) are not only edible but very good to eat. A pumpkin vine usually puts out a very large number of flowers, surplus to requirement. Pick the male flowers just as they are about to open (leaving the female flowers to produce the pumpkins). They are best eaten as fritters, deep-fried in batter with or without herbs and any other embellishments. They can also be stuffed with cheese or minced prawns—anything your imagination fancies—before being deep-fried. In Chinese cooking, the flowers make a colourful contribution when stir-fried in combination with other vegetables such as bamboo shoots, Chinese cabbage, snow peas and so forth.

PURSLANE (Pigweed) 松葉牡丹 / 馬齒莧 | *Portulaca oleracea*

Although purslane has a long history of cultivation and is a common food plant in the Middle East, and some parts of Europe, locally it is regarded as a troublesome weed. I have never seen it on sale anywhere, although I read in a Chinese periodical that it is sometimes sold in the New Territories by little old ladies who forage for it on the hillsides. Some construction workers passing by my garden one day also told me that it is fairly easily obtainable in markets in China where it commands a good price. However, I have never seen it served as food outside of my own home. The species name is a giveaway: *oleracea* means "cultivated or eaten as food". Its common name "pigweed" is also informative: it is used sometimes for pig feed.

The plant is a low-growing, sprawling, succulent herb, about 10 cm high, with fleshy green leaves, sometimes with purple tones. Its flowers are tiny, yellow and not unattractive. Purslane appears all over my garden, uninvited, and is often found growing in crevices and on roadsides. Most gardeners would rub it out, but I always keep some protected as edible landscaping. You can increase your supply by starting some cuttings in pots in the summer. A few pots will keep you always in stock.

It is best enjoyed eaten raw in salads. It tastes a little bland, but is delightfully crunchy and is always a talking point when I introduce it to friends. Be careful to only harvest from your own garden and not from roadsides where they may have been anointed by passing dogs! Purslane can also be lightly stir-fried, when it resembles spinach, or it can be added to scrambled eggs.

Purslane is reputed to be highly nutritious, packed with vitamin C and minerals. It also contains alpha-linolenic acid, one of the highly sought after omega-3 fatty acids. Spinach also possesses this substance, but purslane has three times as much. It has even caught the attention of the U.S. Department of Agriculture, which has identified purslane as being of special value in its effort to modify the western diet towards more fruit and vegetables. So stay your hand when you are about to yank it out—harvest it and eat it instead!

Purslane

ROSE APPLE (Jambos) 蒲桃 | *Syzygium jambos*

Rose apple is unlikely to interest most urban gardeners as it is not something that is deliberately planted. It is a medium-sized evergreen tree native to India and Malaysia but which is now firmly naturalised in the wild in Hong Kong. I include this because I happen to have such a wild tree within the perimeter of my garden, and I find it interesting. It has dark green, leathery, lanceolate leaves with flowers that resemble cream-coloured powder puffs. The fruit is a pale yellow globe comprising a thin rind enclosing a few seeds within its hollow. The ripe fruit is extremely fragrant and its taste reminiscent of rose water. They are very popular with passers-by who are very welcome to help themselves. Other creatures drawn to the fruit are red squirrels (*Callosciurus erythraeus thai*), though they look mostly grey. A squirrel hanging upside down and munching contentedly away on a fruit is somehow a very comforting sight after a busy day in the city.

This is an attractive tree which I feel needs to be given more recognition: it is easily and inexpensively raised from seed (seedings are found everywhere around the base of the tree), is manageable-sized, is evergreen, and thrives in urban areas with minimal maintenance. I think it has all the requisities of a good roadside tree. Whereas some are already grown in limited locations, it deserves to be more widely planted and would result in considerable savings in cost when compared to planting imported exotics.

A closely related tree, the Java apple (*Syzygium samarangense*) 南洋蒲桃 is cultivated for its fruit in tropical countries such as Thailand. In Hong Kong it is commonly found in the wild, and one such tree grows just below my garden compound. It bears bunches

Rose apple flowers

Java apple

Rose apple

of very attractive cone-shaped, edible (though bland) bright pink fruits that appear in spectacular abundance in the summer. This however would not be suitable as a roadside tree because windfall fruits litter the ground and need to be constantly cleared. This particular point has some of my Nature-blind neighbours very annoyed, most of whom would like to fell this magnificent 25-metre-high tree. In fact, on one occasion I had to rush down to restrain a hired hand from crudely hacking it to pieces.

STERCULIA 假蘋婆 | *Sterculia lanceolata*

This is not a garden plant but rather a small-to-medium-sized evergreen tree found in the wild all over Hong Kong. It flowers in the spring, but is at its most attractive in mid-summer when its spectacular scarlet fruit appears. The fruit is made up of five radiating follicles which split along their lower edges to reveal the hard seeds, the size of small marbles. These are pale to begin with but mature to a jet black. Beneath the thin black surface, a more substantial carapace encloses a fleshy interior not unlike a chestnut. Not many people know that these seeds are edible and that they were once commonly collected for sale in wet markets. With urbanisation, this activity has now virtually disappeared, but they are still not difficult to find in the wild. The seeds are boiled and eaten as a snack.

Sterculia fruit

Sterculia seeds

SUNFLOWER 向日葵 | *Helianthus annus*

A common sight in China is people snacking on sunflower seeds. Its origin though, is from North America, one of the few food crop species to emerge from that part of the world. As one of the world's most important oilseeds, sunflowers are grown over huge tracts on all continents. What greater a feast for the eyes than a field of sunflowers stretching to the horizon! These are the tall, even gigantic plants 3 m tall and not the tinkered versions made more compact for the garden. Because of their size, these plants are happiest in the ground, but good-sized sunflowers can be successfully grown in a large pot, for example a 50-litre urn. Grow them in the autumn in October or in the spring, in March. Flowerhead sizes of 25 cm are achievable. They usually do not need support, but they can be susceptible to high winds so do not hesitate to stake them if necessary.

Sunflowers

Sunflower head: *phyllotaxis*

Sunflower seeds

About 80% of the sunflower crop is used for oil used in cooking, salads and for making margarine. The oil is valued for its light colour and high level of unsaturated fatty acids.

But to be perfectly honest, I grow sunflowers not so much for the seeds but for the magnificence and majesty of the flowers. Besides, the home gardener is not likely to see many edible seeds. For good pollination, sunflowers must be grown closely packed and in large numbers (cf. "Sweet corn"). Only then can one expect a harvest of edible seeds. Examine closely a flower head and admire how the phyllotactic design creates an intricate criss-crossing pattern. The numbers of seeds in the succeeding clockwise/anticlockwise spirals turn out to be Fibonacci numbers—fascinating!

SWEET POTATO SHOOTS 番薯苗 | *Ipomoea batatas*

Sweet potato shoots

Eating sweet potato shoots is just about as far as you can get from nouvelle cuisine. This is a rough-and-ready countrified dish that would be scorned by gourmets. They would be missing something. There are many uses for the tubers, but not many people would know how to use the leaves. Only the terminal shoots are used, with two or three attached leaves. The rest of the plant would be too fibrous to eat. They are best prepared by light stir-frying, still retaining some of its crispness. It tastes and looks like Chinese spinach. Once, in a vegetarian restaurant, I ordered sweet potato shoots. The kitchen had run out of it and without letting me know, I was brought Chinese spinach instead. They thought I would not notice, but I was not to be fooled. One other way of preparing these shoots is to make a salad combined with shallots, as it is made in the Philippines. See the recipe section.

WILD EGGPLANT 野矮瓜 | *Solanum torvum*

Wild eggplant

Those familiar with Thai cuisine will have noticed what look like green peas in their curries. These are in fact tiny fruits known as wild eggplant or pea eggplant. These come from a large, sprawling, thorny shrub extremely common in the wild in Hong Kong. I was first drawn to this fact some years ago whilst hiking, when I found a young Thai girl scrambling over one such bush, collecting the tiny fruit. Puzzled, I questioned her about what she was collecting and received some instant education about eggplant. Fruits gathered in the wild are quite safe to eat.

WILD CHINESE SPINACH 野莧/馬屎莧 | *Amaranthus viridis*

Many, many years ago I was introduced to wild spinach by my much-missed Chinese amah who served it to me in a soup. It is gathered in the wild and can occasionally be found in wet markets hawked together with other fresh traditional Chinese herbs. Generally though, it is considered a rampant and troublesome summer weed.

Wild Chinese spinach

Once present in your garden, it revisits every summer. The plant is a much-branched herb growing to 20 cm. The grey-green leaves are ovate and tiny flowers appear tightly bunched in axillary and terminal panicles. The plant is best harvested just before the flowers appear as older plants have very fibrous stems. It may be stir-fried, but its best use is in a soup, either a light quick soup or a more hearty version combined with tofu and fish. Just like purslane, I always leave some wild spinach in my garden as edible landscaping.

WOOD EAR FUNGUS (Jew's ear, Jelly ear) 木耳

Auricularia auricula-judae

The wood ear fungus is one type of jelly fungus that is commonly found growing on dead wood and branches. I often find it in my garden in neglected, damp, dark corners where old wood or logs have been left unattended. The wood ear fungus is distinguished by its ear-like shape, greyish-brown coloration, and a rubbery, gelatinous texture with a whitish bloom. A near relative, the cloud ear fungus (*A. polytricha*) 雲耳 is very similar though somewhat more delicate in structure. Wood ear occurs worldwide in temperate climates. It is usually sold in the dried form and is a popular ingredient in Chinese cuisine, being used in stir-fries, hot and sour soup, snake soup and so forth. Wood ear is also used in traditional medicine for sore throats, jaundice and as an astringent. It is claimed to have anti-tumour, hypoglycaemic, anticoagulant and cholesterol-lowering properties.

Wood ear fungus

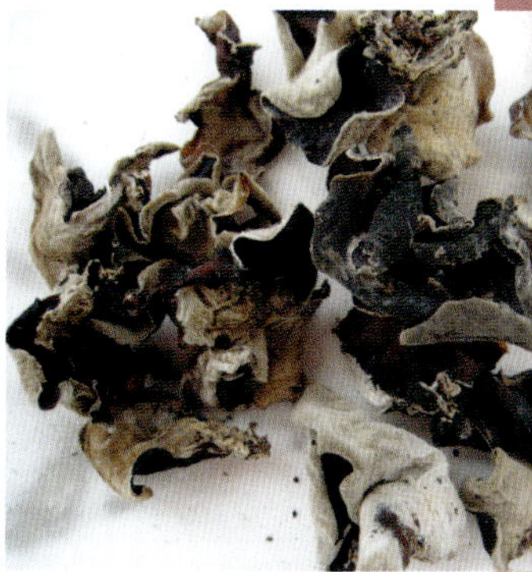
Dried wood ear fungus

YOU GREW IT, NOW LET'S EAT!

"... this emotion of wonder filled me for each vegetable as it was gathered every year. There is nothing that is comparable to it, as satisfactory or as thrilling, as gathering the vegetables one has grown."

—*The Alice B. Toklas Cookbook* (1954)

A YEAR OF NATURE'S PLENTY

A year of well-planned planting results in a year of continual harvesting. Here are some of my favourites which never fail to delight, year after year. Remember almost all of these items can be grown in containers.

January

This is a wonderful month with cold crisp weather and the greatest likelihood of clear skies. The kitchen garden should be practically at its best, with winter crops ready for harvesting. The leafy Chinese vegetables such as kai lan, choi sum and pak choi are ready for cutting. Lettuce of all kinds are in their prime as well as all the other ingredients for a tasty salad: tomatoes, celery, carrots, cicoria, capsicum. One of my favourite pickings at this time would be a beautiful, fat and crisp cabbage. White radish can be pulled up and used for loh pak koh, a favourite dish around the Chinese New Year season.

February

February would still offer all of the above, although some signs of decline may be evident. Humidity will be rising and such crops as tomatoes will be past their best. Still there should be no shortage of salad vegetables. Late winter sowings of kohl rabi and bell peppers are best at this time and should continue until next month. Carrots and beets should still be available. This would be about the time to think of what one should do about summer crops. Plant sweet corn and peanuts.

March

March marks the start of the "in-between" season, when winter crops are coming to an end and when it is too early for summer vegetables. This is a good time for vegetables that can manage to do well in this odd period, for example kai choi is a timely stopgap crop as well as kohl rabi as mentioned above.

A second sowing of white radish in December will provide further pickings this month. If green vegetables are in short supply, sweet potato shoots can be harvested if you have some growing. Actually these shoots are useful any time of the year when the going gets tough. Potatoes planted in January can be dug up, and parsnips, if you have grown them, should be ready. This is the time to start all kinds of squashes and beans. Strawberries should be ripening and continuing into the following month.

April

Rain may be starting up, though seldom torrential. Lettuce will be running low, but the lesser known fu muk choi (*Lactuca chinensis*) is an excellent stand-in. In fact, it will perform this function throughout the summer and can be used raw in salads or stir-fried. Hot chillies should be plentiful and this is a good time to make chilli sauce. Some herbs such as parsley and coriander will have died out, but basil, rosemary and mint should still be in good supply. Lemongrass grows year-round. The weather should be warming up and as soon as the night-time temperature remains above 20°C start planting okra. Also a good time to start eggplant. The summer Chinese greens especially water spinach, Chinese spinach and Ceylon spinach should almost be ready for cutting.

May

The Chinese greens mentioned under April will be at their best but rain can be expected at any time and Chinese spinach is vulnerable in heavy downpours. Water spinach will revel in the wet. Beans and various types of squash and pumpkins are harvested. Sweet corn should be nearly ready. Sugar cane, a year-round crop, can be cut to prepare an icy-cold summer drink. Papayas, looking miserable right after winter will now be picking up and both green and ripe fruit may be enjoyed and continue to be enjoyed well into autumn.

June

What is expected in May will continue through June. It is still too soon for typhoons ("June: too soon") to cause mischief. Figs will be appearing and the shrubs should be growing lustily. Enjoy a freshly picked ear of sweet corn. Okra should be appearing on the plants.

July

Typhoons can be expected to hit at any time. However, all the summer vegetables will do well between the storms. Careful sequential sowing should maintain a supply well into September. Okra production will be in full swing to the delight of curry lovers. This is my favourite summer crop and I grow enough to freeze to enjoy another day. Eggplants starting production. Sweet potatoes may be dug up after flowering. This can be done every few months throughout the year.

August

The hardest time of the year to work in the garden with the searing heat taking a toll on both the gardener and the plants. Roof gardens are especially susceptible, but all summer vegetables continue to perform.

September

Hopes begin to rise for a respite from scorching summer heat. However, changes in the climate pattern have meant that it does not really begin to cool until the end of the month. Fruits such as pomelo, avocado, wampi, lemon and figs may be enjoyed. A bumper harvest of okras and eggplants will allow you to experiment with new recipes. Avoid sowing winter vegetables until there is a distinct autumnal cooling. However, tomatoes may be given an earlier start so as to be ready for Christmas.

October

There should by now be a definite lowering of temperatures and the whole array of winter vegetables may be sown. Sow snow and sugar peas a little later as they do really need cool weather. This is a major make-over time in the garden and more attention should be paid to starting plants than to harvesting although the tail end of summer vegetables will still provide some meals.

November

A busy month taking stock and dealing with seedlings, transplanting and setting out of plants. The earliest winter green to reach the table should be chrysanthemum vegetable. This is one of the easiest vegetables to grow and cutting can begin in four or five weeks. Succesive sowings will keep up the supply for the next four or five months. Another equally speedy result can be expected from radish.

December

Everything started at the end of September or the beginning of October will be showing promise and many, such as tomatoes and lettuce, will make a welcome return to the dining table. Towards the end of the month, Christmas can be celebrated with just about everything started a few months ago. A good time to show off your luxuriant garden to friends.

Having grown your own food, the next pleasurable step is to prepare it for the table. I am no gourmet, but I enjoy a wide range of food, mostly home and hearty country fare. Some of the recipes reveal my Macanese upbringing and reflect some things I learnt from my mother who was a talented cook. A few of the recipes cater to an acquired taste and some may be unusual. Enjoy!

Batatada (Macanese Sweet Potato Pudding)

This pudding is little known outside of Macao or Hong Kong's dwindling Macanese community. This recipe comes courtesy of a good friend who is a well-known local Macanese cook.

Ingredients

- 1 kg yellow-fleshed sweet potatoes
- 200 g butter or margarine
- 1½ cups sugar
- 400 ml canned coconut milk (preferably OSC brand)
- 4 whole eggs
- 6 egg yolks
- ½ cup plain flour
- ½ cup corn starch
- 1 tbsp vanilla essence

Method

- Line a cake pan with double-duty aluminium foil and brush the bottom and sides with vegetable oil.
- Cook the sweet potatoes until soft and peel. Mash the potatoes while still hot, adding the sugar and butter or margarine, mixing thoroughly.
- Cool the mixture slightly, sift in the flour and corn starch separately, then add the coconut milk.
- Beat the eggs and yolks lightly with a fork, then add the vanilla essence.
- Add the egg mixture to the potato mixture and blend thoroughly until smooth. A blender can be used for this step.
- Pour the whole mixture into the lined pan and bake at medium heat until done—about 90 minutes.
- Serve chilled or at room temperature.

Caldo Verde (Portuguese Green Soup)

This is a classic, the most popular of all Portuguese soups. Everyone has a slightly different way of preparing it. Traditionally, kale is used, but the rough, green, outer leaves of a cabbage may be used instead. Here is my version, with apologies to the purists!

Ingredients

- 4 medium potatoes
- 100 g kale or green cabbage leaves
- 2 bay leaves
- 1.5 litres water
- 100 g Portuguese pork sausage, thinly sliced
- 2 tbsp extra virgin olive oil
- 1 tbsp evaporated milk
- salt and pepper
- 200 ml chicken broth (optional)

Method

- Peel and roughly quarter the potatoes.
- Using 1 litre of the water, cook the potatoes until soft. Do not discard the water.
- Blend the potatoes using the remaining 0.5 litres of water.
- Return to the pot and simmer for 10 minutes.
- Meanwhile roll up the kale or cabbage leaves and slice very finely.
- Add the vegetables and sausage, and optional chicken broth, and simmer for a further 10 minutes.
- Stir in the evaporated milk and the olive oil and serve.
- Bom apetite !

Celtuce Salad

Celtuce is a novelty to most people. Only the stems of the celtuce are eaten. This unusual but simple salad never fails to draw compliments.

Ingredients

- 4–5 celtuce stems
- 15 ml sesame oil
- 2 tbsp salt

Method

- Peel the celtuce stems, reaching fairly deeply to remove all traces of fibre. Wash and pat dry.
- Slice the stems into ovals about 0.5 cm thick and add the salt.
- Place the sliced celtuce into a colander, then cover completely with a plate.
- Place a heavy weight (about 2 kg) onto the plate and leave for 1 hour. A fair amount of water will be extracted by the combined action of the salt and the heavy weight.
- Remove the celtuce and pat dry. Adjust the taste with extra salt if necessary and mix in the sesame oil.
- Serve cold.

Chilli Sauce 辣椒醬

A little heat enhances some dishes by complementing without overwhelming. Locally-bought chilli sauces are mostly pretty good, but making your own puts your stamp on a delicious product.

Ingredients

- 250 g hot chillies, finely chopped
- 3 cloves garlic, finely chopped
- 50 g dried shrimps 蝦米
- 1 dried scallop
- 1 tbsp 5-spice powder 五香粉
- 200 ml peanut oil
- 50 ml sesame oil
- 30 ml light soy sauce

Method

- Soak the scallop and the dried shrimps in tepid water until soft (about 3 hours), then drain and finely mince.
- Sauté the minced scallop and shrimps in a little peanut oil, over low heat (about 5 minutes).
- Mix in the garlic, chillies, soy sauce, sesame oil and 5-spice powder and continue to stir-fry on low heat.
- From time to time, add a tablespoonful of peanut oil until the full quota is used up, in about 20 minutes.
- Cool the finished product and store in small bottles to distribute to your favourite people.

Chinese Quick Soups 滾清湯

Chinese home cooking makes use of some very simple and quick soups, light and healthy, usually without meat, sometimes with added (soft) tofu or egg white, etc. All of these soups are made by blanching the vegetables in boiling water for 5 minutes or so, adding salt and pepper to taste, a knob of ginger and any of the complementary ingredients listed below. The addition of some chicken broth is optional.

Vegetable	Other added ingredients (optional)
capsicum leaves	tofu
Ceylon spinach	tofu
Chinese cabbage	vermicelli/tofu
hairy or silk squash	vermicelli
lettuce	tofu
matrimony vine	tofu/egg white/pork liver
mustard (kai choi)	salted duck egg
string bean leaves	tofu
wild spinach	tofu/fish

Chinese Stir-Fried Vegetables 炒菜

Stir-fried vegetables is a Chinese invention. The vegetables are cooked *au jus* and not done to death. However, to bring out every advantage, each vegetable in a stir-fry needs to be matched with garlic or ginger. Which one to use? Here is my answer.

Garlic	Ginger
beans (various)	asparagus
cabbage	broccoli
cauliflower	kai lan
Chinese spinach	lettuce
choi sum	mustard (kai choi)
chrysanthemum vegetable	pak choi
kohl rabi	
pea shoots	
snow peas	
spinach	
squash (various)	
water spinach	
white radish	

Cold Sweet Potato Leaves Salad

This is a Filipino dish, refreshing on a hot summer's day. It is new to most people I serve it to. This menu is courtesy of our helpers Mary and Cynthia.

Ingredients

- 250 g fresh sweet potato leaves (tender shoots only)
- 3 shallots
- 3 tbsp balsamic vinegar
- 2 tbsp olive oil
- salt and sugar to taste

Method

- Blanch the leaves in boiling water for 1 minute.
- Remove and rinse immediately with cold water.
- Lightly sauté the sliced shallots and the sweet potato leaves.
- Cool the salad, drizzle with the balsamic vinegar and olive oil and serve cold.

Crabs with Papaya Flowers

This typical Macanese dish makes use of what is now an increasingly rare commodity: papaya flowers from the male tree.

Ingredients

- 1 kg medium-sized crabs
- large handful of male papaya flowers, up to 400 g
- 1 large knob ginger, sliced
- 1 chopped medium-sized red chilli
- 2 tbsp balichao* 鹹蝦醬
- 30 ml Chinese rice wine
- 1 tbsp turmeric powder
- 1 sprig fresh coriander
- salt and pepper to taste

Method

- Wash and chop up the crabs, cracking the shell of the claws with a large chopper.
- Blanch the papaya flowers in boiling water for 2–3 minutes to remove the excess bitterness. (Taste the blanched flowers to determine if the degree of bitterness is acceptable.)
- Stir-fry the ginger, turmeric and balichao.
- Add the crabs, the blanched flowers and the wine, cover the pan with a lid and cook for 5 minutes.
- Garnish with coriander and chopped chilli.

* Balichao 鹹蝦醬 is a shrimp sauce which is difficult to obtain. Chinese shrimp paste may be used as a substitute.

Fig Syrup

This is not something you can buy in shops. The only source I know is the Carmelite Convent in Stanley, where the sisters produce a limited quantity for sale. If you are able to source fresh fig leaves, it is not difficult to make your own. On a hot summer's day, a drink prepared from the syrup is wonderfully soothing.

Ingredients

- 40 fresh fig leaves
- 3 kg rock sugar
- white and shell of one egg
- 6 litres water

Method

- Boil the leaves in 6 litres of water for 1 hour.
- Remove the leaves, then add 3 kg rock sugar and simmer until completely dissolved.
- Sieve the liquid to remove any sediments.
- Add the white of one egg together with the egg shell. A light scum that forms on the surface will cling to the egg white and shell, which can then be scooped away.
- Simmer for about 5 hours or as long as it takes to reach the consistency and colour of honey.
- To drink, mix 30 ml of the syrup in a glass of water, add ice and serve.

Green Tomato Chutney

At the end of the growing season, spent tomato plants need to be disposed of. But at this time there is often a surfeit of green, unripe tomatoes which are usually discarded. A wonderful way to make use of these tomatoes is to turn them into delicious chutney. The recipe is a simplified version, dispensing with the need for overnight preparation as traditional methods demand. Green tomato chutney makes a great accompaniment for cheese, roasts, pork chops, hot dogs and so forth.

Ingredients

- 1 kg green tomatoes, roughly chopped
- 1 medium onion, finely chopped
- 1 small apple, cored, peeled and roughly chopped
- 1 cup sultanas, roughly chopped
- 1 cup brown sugar
- 1 cup cider vinegar
- 1 tsp salt

Method

- Combine all the ingredients in a heavy-bottomed pot.
- Bring to a boil, then reduce to simmer for one hour.
- Check for consistency—a jam-like thickness is the ideal.
- Continue simmering if necessary to achieve the desired result.
- Check for taste and enjoy.

Margoso Lorcha (Macanese Stuffed Bitter Squash)

The lorcha was a fast sailing vessel, designed in Macao, with a western-style hull and Chinese rigging. A bitter squash (margoso), when split down the middle, presents us with two boat-shaped halves. With the pulp scooped out, it resembles a boat or "lorcha"—a perfect vehicle for stuffing.

Ingredients

- 3 medium-sized bitter squashes
- 250 g minced pork
- 1 medium onion
- 2 tbsp balichao 鹹蝦醬 (or Chinese shrimp paste)
- 1 tbsp light soy sauce
- 1 sprig fresh coriander
- 4 cloves garlic, chopped
- 2 tbsp cornflour
- 1 can chopped tomatoes
- salt and pepper

Method

- Dice the onion and fry in a little vegetable oil until soft.
- Prepare and marinade the stuffing combining the minced pork, soy sauce, fried onion and a pinch of cornflour.
- Cut the squashes into two halves, scoop out the pulp and blanch in boiling salted water for 1 minute. Discard the water.
- Fill the shells or "lorchas" with the stuffing.
- Fry the lorchas stuffing side down until brown, then set aside.
- Prepare the sauce—fry the garlic, tomatoes and balichao, adding the cornflour mixed with 4 tablespoons of water to thicken the sauce, then pour over the stuffed lorchas, and simmer for a further 15 minutes.

Mustard Green Pickles 辣菜

These sweet-sour, crunchy pickles are a cinch to prepare and can be kept in the refrigerator for a month.

Ingredients

- 1 kai choi heart (Swatow variety) 大芥菜
- 300 ml white distilled vinegar
- 300 g rock sugar
- 1 tbsp Coleman's mustard powder
- 1 knob ginger, sliced
- 3 hot red chillies

Method

- Trim the kai choi hearts by removing the outer leaves, using only the petioles.
- Cut into pieces about 3 cm by 3 cm. Wash and lay aside.
- Heat the vinegar, ginger and sugar in a pan over low heat until the sugar is completely dissolved.
- Stir in the mustard and allow to cool.
- Add the kai choi pieces and the chillies and transfer to a suitable bottle.
- The pickles should be ready to eat in 48 hours.

Okra and Minced Beef (or Lamb) Curry

This is by far my favourite way to use okras, so plentiful in the summer. A simple curry whipped up in a jiffy.

Ingredients

- 15 whole okras
- 400 g minced beef or lamb
- 2 medium onions, chopped
- 2 tbsp tomato paste
- knob of tamarind about walnut-size
- 3 cloves garlic
- knob of ginger
- 3 dried red chillies
- 2 tbsp garam marsala
- 1 tbsp cumin powder
- 1 tbsp coriander powder
- 1 tbsp brown sugar (or Chinese brown bar sugar)
- 2 sprigs curry leaves

Method

- Soak the tamarind in a bowl of warm water for half an hour. Then knead the tamarind to form a thin paste.
- Fry the onions, garlic, ginger and chillies in some vegetable oil until the onions soften.
- Add the garam marsala, cumin and coriander powder, and sauté briefly, taking care not to burn the spices.
- Add the tomato paste, curry leaves, sugar and minced meat. Add the tamarind through a strainer and then cover with water.
- Cook for 20 minutes.
- Add the okras and cook for another 15 minutes, add salt to taste.

Papaya Soup 木瓜湯

Papaya is such a wonderful resource, enjoyed in many ways. Here is one way to make good use of half-ripened papaya. Green papaya is also suitable.

Ingredients

- 1 papaya 300–500 g cut into chunks
- 250 g pork ribs
- 1 knob ginger, sliced
- 6 dried Chinese dates 蜜棗
- small handful of pearl barley

Method

- Blanch the pork ribs with boiling water.
- Stir fry the ginger in a little vegetable oil. Add the ribs and toss briefly. Add the papaya, barley and dates, and simmer for 3 hours and serve. Note that if kept overnight, the flavour improves considerably.

Pesto

One of the greatest pleasures of growing basil is to be able to make fresh pesto. Shop-bought bottled pesto does not compare. This classic Italian sauce brings life to any pasta dish. It will also complement meat dishes and can be used as a dip.

Ingredients

- 4 handfuls of fresh basil, roughly chopped
- 4 cloves garlic, peeled
- 1 cup pine nuts or walnuts
- 1 cup grated Parmesan cheese
- 1 cup extra virgin olive oil
- salt and pepper

Method

- Toast the pine nuts in a frying pan until golden brown.
- Put all the ingredients in a blender and blend at a low speed while gradually adding the olive oil. Add as much olive oil as is needed to bring the mixture to your desired consistency. Use immediately. Any remainder can be stored in the refrigerator for a week. If intended for longer than this, put in the freezer. However, it is best to make just enough for your present needs and to make fresh batches as required.

Sugar Cane Drink 蔗水

This is what I grow my sugar cane for! It is simplicity itself to prepare and can be served iced or hot, depending on the season. If served hot, the retained heat in the canes will keep the drink warm for several hours.

Ingredients

- 2 lengths of sugar cane, each about 1.5 m long
- 250 g rock sugar
- 5 litres water

Method

- Cut the canes into lengths of about 15 cm, peel and pulverise with a few sharp blows using the back of a stout chopper.
- Boil the canes in the water for 2 hours.
- Add the rock sugar and simmer until completely dissolved.

Sweet Potato Dessert 番薯糖水

A quick, simple traditional dessert.

Ingredients

- 400 g sweet potato, peeled and cut into small chunks
- 1 slab unrefined Chinese bar sugar (about 80 g)
- 5 thick slices ginger (about 20 g)
- 1 litre water

Method

- Boil the water with the sugar and ginger until the sugar is dissolved. Skim off any scum that may have risen from the sugar.
- Add the sweet potato and keep on the boil for 30 minutes or until the potato has softened.
- Serves 4, hot or cold.

White Radish Pudding 蘿蔔糕

This classic Chinese pudding is a perennial favourite, best appreciated at Chinese New Year time when it is consumed in great quantities. Once again, freshly made pudding is the way to go. The consistency needs to be just right so that it can be sliced, yet must not be too firm.

Ingredients

- 3.5 kg white radish, peeled
- 500 g non-glutinous rice flour 粘米粉
- 4 Chinese sausages, chopped into 1 cm bits
- 50 g dried shrimps 蝦米
- 250 g minced pork (or canned luncheon meat)
- 2 tbsp 5-spice powder 五香粉
- 1 bunch coriander, chopped
- salt and pepper
- 2 tbsp white sugar
- for garnish: toasted sesame seeds, chopped spring onions, sprigs of fresh coriander

Method

- Finely shred the radish with a chopper or a shredder. Do not use a blender.
- Cook the radish in a large pot (without adding oil or water) until just soft: about 10 minutes.
- Add the minced pork and cook for another 5 minutes. If luncheon meat is used, it should first be sliced, fried, and then chopped before adding to the shredded radish.
- Remove from the heat, and stir in the rice flour, Chinese sausages, dried shrimps, 5-spice powder, chopped coriander, salt and pepper.
- Mix all the ingredients very thoroughly, then transfer the pasty mixture into suitable pans and steam for at least 60 minutes or until the correct consistency is reached.
- Garnish with chopped spring onions and coriander sprigs and sprinkle with toasted sesame seeds. Cool before slicing and serve fresh. The pudding can be kept for about 1 week in the refrigerator. Cold slices are best browned in a frying pan before serving.
- Enjoy with some of your homemade chilli sauce.

BIBLIOGRAPHY

Bibliography

- *Botanica*, 2nd edition. Australia: Random House, 1998.
- *British National Formulary 67*. London: BMJ Group and Pharmaceutical Press, 2014.
- *Desk Reference to Nature's Medicine*. Steven Foster and Rebecca L. Johnson. Washington D.C.: National Geographic Society, 2006.
- *Encyclopaedia of Vegetables and Fruits in Taiwan (1)* 台灣蔬果實用百科1. 薛聰賢編著. 台灣: 台灣普綠有限公司, 2000.
- *Flora of Hong Kong* Vols 1–3. Hong Kong Herbarium and South China Botanical Garden. Hong Kong: Agriculture Fisheries and Conservation Department, 2007/2008/2009.
- *Food, Nutrition, Physical Activity, and the Prevention of Cancer: A Global Perspective*. Washington D. C.: World Cancer Research Fund/American Institute for Cancer Research, 2007.
- *Food Plants of China*. Hu Shiu-ying. Hong Kong: The Chinese University Press, 2005.
- *Food Plants of the World*. Ben-Erik van Wyk. Portland: Timber Press, 2005.
- *Gardener's Latin*. Bill Neal. Chapel Hill: Algonquin Books, 1992.
- *Gardening for Hong Kong*. W.J. Tutcher, 1913. Hong Kong: Reprinted by *South China Morning Post*, 1964.
- *Grow Organic!* Kadoorie Farm and Botanic Garden. Hong Kong: Wan Li Book Co. Ltd., 2007.
- *Hong Kong Food Plants*. S.Y. Zee and L.H. Hui. Hong Kong: Urban Council, 1981.
- *RHS Latin for Gardeners*. Lorraine Harrison. London: Mitchell Beazley, 2012.
- *Slow Food Almanac*. The Internationial Slow Food Association, 2008.
- *The Hong Kong Countryside*. G.A.C. Herklots. Hong Kong: *South China Morning Post*, 1951.
- *The One Straw Revolution*. Masanobu Fukuoka. New York: New York Review of Books edition, 2009.
- *Urban Gardening: A Hong Kong Gardener's Journal*. Arthur van Langenberg. Hong Kong: The Chinese University Press, 2006.

ACKNOWLEDGEMENTS

Acknowledgements

The opportunity to prepare an expanded edition of *Growing Your Own Food in Hong Kong* came as a pleasant surprise and allowed me to collaborate once again with The Chinese University Press. Alterations and additions to an existing manuscript is an endeavour to test the patience and skills of the publishers to produce a seamless result. The team comprising Angelina Wong, Kingsley Ma, Daniel Ng and Joyce Liu accomplished this task effortlessly, while making the whole process a very enjoyable one. My sincere thanks to them.

My wife Nim Yin—a constant presence in the garden—is found somewhere in every page of this book. Thanks.

WHAT GARDERNERS SAY ...

What Gardeners Say ...

Timely and topical, Arthur van Langenberg's new edition of his unique book is this Hong Kong doctor's manual to healthy growing and eating and complements current opinions on sustainable food cultivation—a view supported by the UN Farming Report, "Wake Up Before It's Too Late" (2013), which finds that the answer to feeding the world is organic and small scale farming rather than monocultures and GMOs.

Not long ago, households could be assured of fresh home-grown vegetables from their own makeshift patch or villagers via local markets. Today, there is food aplenty but food scares are commonplace. Cultivating your own produce requires determination, ingenuity, the skills of a gardener and Arthur's guidance in this book.

Despite land hungry policies eradicating agriculture, there is a burgeoning community push for home-grown produce to experience the pleasures of production and harvest, to have control over their food, to lessen human impact on the planet, for waste to be composted, food to be local and not delivered by planes, for eating seasonally, safely, and for food to be better tasting and more nutritious.

Community gardens on government land are increasing but plots are only held for a few months and allocated on a lucky draw system. The trend elsewhere is for whole communities to be growing more of their own food. Yet, much of Hong Kong's agricultural land is not farmed but held for property speculation and not protected against degradation and pollution. Such issues are being discussed locally and already there are high-rise gardens in the form of factory-building and roof-top gardens.

Forward thinking decision makers must integrate agriculture into our urban landscape, into or beside buildings, instead of just permitting more buildings! Success will require the information, advice and wisdom gained through years of experience of cultivating food plants in our urban conditions contained in this fascinating volume.

Karen Barretto
Conservationist gardener

Arthur is so much ahead of us organic growers. In fact, he has been growing vegetables and herbs organically at his home micro-garden for over 30 years. Since we are always told that "we are what we eat", Arthur takes you through an entire experience of "you eat what you grow" and furthermore "at your own home". He shares with you the basics of gardening as city dwellers from propagating seeds, composting and soil management, and pest control to harvesting your own food and the details of when, where and how to tackle difficulties and achieve better results. He also offers simple recipes for home cooking, allowing you to appreciate the process of learning about where our food comes from and to enjoy the wonderful tastes arising from the labours of passion.

Pui-Kwan Chu
Founder of the Organic Farm, 1995
Urban farming and edible education advocate

Growing Your Own Food in Hong Kong is a rare and commendable hybrid. The book goes beyond a gardener's manual to include health advice. Arthur goes on to philosophise about how disconnected we are due to the commercialisation and industrialisation of food processing; and advocates a return to basics. The nostalgia of a much more organic society is presented through snippets of Arthur's recollection—that of his Chinese amah serving him soup made with wild edible plants, and insights of the food culture of bygone days adds a humane dimension. Arthur is an experienced gardener and his pages are strewn with practical advice, botanical and gardening knowledge; complete with well-tested family recipes. This book is invaluable to anyone looking for a gardening mentor.

Sylvia Midgett
Chair, The Hong Kong Gardening Society

開始有機耕種時，要搜羅關於香港種植的書，真有如大海撈針。幸好我找到 Arthur 的書。他的書對新手和專業人士都非常有用。我初從事有機耕種時，心情戰戰兢兢，因為我連一顆種子也沒觸摸過。而 Arthur 的書簡單易明，圖文並茂，在我對有機農業懷有夢想的初期，給我很大幫助。它不但製作嚴謹，更有多種「東西共融」的品種，讓我從中受到很多啟發，並一直從事有機耕種至今。我很期待 Arthur 的新書。

如今在我的農場裏，既有本地的品種，亦種植多種「異國風情」的蔬果。它們為市場/消費者提供更多農產品的選擇；而外國名廚既驚訝西方蔬果能在本地培植，亦從東方蔬果獲得不少靈感，為香港這個「美食天堂」加添新元素。香港人口福真不淺！

希望更多的香港人能在家中窗台、陽台種植自家蔬菜。有機耕種不但帶來更健康美味的食物，讓你與親朋戚友共享這喜悅，或許更會改變你的生命。

Joey Ng
Zen Organic Farm

Most people in Hong Kong will consider growing their own food a fantasy. It can become reality with the help of this invaluable book. It exudes energy and passion and provides simple, down-to-earth advice on how best to start a hobby which can soon turn into a way of life. Children and adults alike will discover the joys of watching plants grow before eating them, be it a few herbs on a window sill in a small flat or a handful of potatoes in a pot on a balcony. And once you are hooked there is no stopping you.

Jacqueline Hampshire
Membership Secretary, The Hong Kong Gardening Society

INDEX OF PLANT NAMES

Index of Plant Names

	JANUARY	FEBRUARY	MARCH	APRIL
PLANTING TIMELINE	Arugula, beetroot, broccoli, capsicum, carrot, cauliflower, choi sum, chrysanthemum vegetable, kai choi, kai lan, kohl rabi, lettuce, pak choi, potato, radish, spinach, Swiss chard, watercress	Capsicum (bell pepper), chrysanthemum vegetable, kai choi, lettuce (fu muk choi), peanut, sweet corn	Basil, beans (all kinds except broad beans), capsicum (bell pepper), Chinese spinach, chrysanthemum vegetable, cucumber, kai choi, lettuce (fu muk choi), peanut, squashes (including pumpkins & melons), sweet corn	Basil, beans (all kinds except broad beans), capsicum (hot chilli), Ceylon spinach, Chinese spinach, cucumber, eggplant, ginger, kai choi, okra, peanut, squashes (including pumpkins & melons), sweet corn, sweet potato, turmeric, water spinach

HARVEST TIMELINE	Arugula, beetroot, broad beans, broccoli, Brussels sprouts, cabbage, capsicum, carrot, celery, Chinese cabbage, choi sum, chrysanthemum vegetable, cicoria, coriander, dill, eggplant, Italian parsley, kai choi, kai lan, kohl rabi, lettuce, nasturtium, pak choi, pea shoots, potato, radish, snow peas, spinach, strawberry, sugar peas, sweet corn, Swiss chard, tomato, turnip, watercress, white radish	Arugula, beetroot, broad beans, broccoli, Brussels sprouts, cabbage, capsicum, carrot, cauliflower, celery, Chinese cabbage, choi sum, chrysanthemum vegetable, coriander, dill, Italian parsley, kai choi, kai lan, kohl rabi, lettuce, nasturtium, oregano, pak choi, pea shoots, potato, radish, sage, snow peas, spinach, strawberry, sugar peas, Swiss chard, taro, thyme, tomato, watercress, white radish	Arugula, beetroot, broccoli, cabbage, capsicum, carrot, cauliflower, celery, Chinese cabbage, choi sum, chrysanthemum vegetable, cicoria, coriander, dill, garlic, Italian parsley, kai choi, kai lan, kohl rabi, lettuce, nasturtium, oregano, pak choi, parsnip, sage, spinach, strawberry, Swiss chard, thyme, tomato, watercress, white radish	Capsicum, carrot, celery, Chinese spinach, chrysanthemum vegetable, garlic, kai choi, leek, lettuce (including fu muk choi), nasturtium, strawberry

GROWN AND AVAILABLE THROUGH MOST OF THE YEAR